The Irish Paradox

HOW AND WHY WE ARE SUCH A CONTRADICTORY PEOPLE

The
Irish Paradox

HOW AND WHY WE ARE SUCH
A CONTRADICTORY PEOPLE

Sean Moncrieff

Gill & Macmillan

Gill & Macmillan
Hume Avenue, Park West, Dublin 12
www.gillmacmillanbooks.ie

Design by Make Communication
Print origination by Síofra Murphy
Printed and bound in Nørhaven, Denmark

This book is typeset in Minion 13/18 pt.

5 4 3 2 1

306
———
09415

€ 12.74c

The Author

Sean Moncrieff is a broadcaster and writer. He is the host of *The Moncrieff Show* every weekday afternoon on Newstalk 106-8 FM. He is the author of three novels, *Dublin, The History of Things* and *The Angel of the Streetlamps*, and two non-fiction books, *Stark Raving Rulers: Twenty Minor Despots of the Twenty-First Century* and *God: A User's Guide*.

For Helen

Acknowledgements

Thanks to Conor Nagle and everyone at Gill & Macmillan for being such a pleasure to deal with. Thanks to Caroline for getting me to do this, and thanks to all the journalists, writers, historians and academics whose work I have borrowed from for this book. I hope I have properly credited you all. And if I haven't, I hope you don't notice.

Contents

Chapter 1

Not One Thing
or the Other

Ireland is a stew. It has been for most of its history. The Vikings came, then the Normans, then waves of English and Scots. Millions of Irish people went away and never came back. Then, in the first decade of this century, over 100,000 returned, along with migrants from around Europe, the Americas, Asia – people who by their very presence here have made their own indentations on Irish life and have changed the ether of Irishness. According to the 2011 census, nearly 20 per cent of the population are classified as immigrants. In a decade, Ireland transformed from a homogenous, pale-skinned society to a multi-ethnic one.

Ireland was once a country in thrall to a strict Catholic morality, but within 30 years the power of the church evaporated. We became secular. In 1993, we were one of the last countries in Europe to decriminalise homosexuality. In 2015, we became the first country in the world to vote for same-sex marriage. For many years we were one of the poorest countries in Europe, then we morphed into the second richest nation on earth. For decades we attempted to insulate ourselves from the outside world, then flipped to become one of the most globalised places on the planet.

We've been clever and stupid, principled and corrupt. We can be kind and cruel, guilty of dopey optimism and chronic fatalism. We're friendly, but near impossible to get to know. We peddle myths to ourselves and to anyone else prepared to listen to them in the hope that the myths prove to be true. We're proud to be Irish but often crippled with self-loathing. We think we're great, but not really.

We find ourselves fascinating.

Of course we do. We're a paradox.

That's what we're looking at in this book: the contradictory, mutating nature of Irishness. Because if there is one constant of our national character, it's uncertainty. We're never quite sure what kind of people we are.

I'm part of this stew. I'm Irish, and like a lot of Irish people I was born in England. The first place I remember is 60 Cobbold Road in Willesden, northwest London. My father was born in Edinburgh and my mother was from Killala in County Mayo. For the times, they were an unlikely match. He was from a Protestant family while my mother was the most ardent sort of Irish Catholic. But perhaps these differences mattered less in a clamorous city where every face was strange.

What they had in common was more important. They had travelled from faraway places where there was a stony acceptance of what today we'd call poverty, but they never would have; other people were poor. Yet it had enough of a dream-crushing quality to prompt them to pack a bag and get on a train. It was life. You got on with it. My father had a childhood memory of coming home to find his baby sister dead, laid out on the dresser. His family home was a dank, Dickensian basement flat on Tron Square in the centre of Edinburgh, where to be male meant being a big drinker and a hard man.

So with a group of others (which briefly included Sean Connery), he headed south to work on building sites beside Scots and Irish and all the other economic refugees.

Dad wasn't, however, extravagant with his recollections. Like my mother, he came from a generation that didn't dwell on past miseries. Even to speak about them was considered weak, or worse, complaining. You got on with it.

Mum was even more closed. From what she occasionally let slip, I have a picture of her as a wistful young girl. She liked to cycle around the Mayo countryside. She read poetry, Yeats: *I will arise and go now.* Yet my sister and I don't know when, or in what circumstances, she travelled to London. Perhaps we should have asked more when they were alive, but they would both reflexively close up in response to any direct questions. *Ah, what do you want to know that for?* The past, or at least the bad bits, didn't need to be remembered.

What we have managed to thread together is that she arrived at some stage during the Second World War. For a time, perhaps during the summer months, she worked as a Clippie – the slang term for female bus conductors. The rest of the time, she taught. After her death we found a job reference stating that Miss O'Reilly came to St Louis High School in Frome, Somerset, in December 1945, where she taught Form 1 boys and girls. She was a good, conscientious teacher, according to the letter, and a popular member of staff. Where she went after that, we don't know. How long she was in the country beforehand is also a mystery. She may have arrived when the war had just ended. She may have seen London in flames.

They were introduced through a mutual friend – an Irishman – courted and (after my father had converted to Catholicism) married. There is a wedding picture of them that sat beside my mother's bed during her final days in the nursing home. They are in the back seat of some chauffeured car, shiny-faced and impossibly young. As far as we know, no family members from either side travelled to the wedding. London was very far away.

Cobbold Road was the first place I remember, though it was not the first place I lived. Before that there was a ground floor flat on Melrose Avenue in Cricklewood, a long road of shabby, late Victorian houses, all of which had been broken up into flats. It later achieved a grim fame for being one of the two places that the serial killer Dennis Nilsen operated from.

My sister Helen, who remembers the Cricklewood flat as dark and a bit scary, can remember travelling back from the hospital in a taxi with our parents and me, the new addition to the family. When we got home, she asked if I would be staying long and when, exactly, they would be taking me back to the hospital.

Not long after that we moved to Willesden. By then my father was working in a factory (a step up from the building site) and there was a general sense in our family of working towards something significant – specifically, house ownership, an achievement that would edge the Moncrieffs from working class to lower middle class. It was our mother who was particularly keen that this happened. She was the one who scrimped and saved and doggedly fought every little financial indulgence. In material terms, her family had been not much better off than my father's, but under the tenets of the unspoken Irish class system, she'd been able to grow up thinking that she was a bit better than that. She'd done the Leaving Certificate, which somehow qualified her to teach in England. To have to live in this part of London – to have to live in England at all – she regarded as an affront.

The houses in Cobbold Road were terraced and red-bricked, though after decades of being smeared in smog the exterior walls resembled the faces of miners emerging from the pit. They were built in the 1880s as part of a furious urbanisation of the area. In the 1960s there were still some Irish living there, along with Poles and Jews, Afro-Caribbeans and Asians. The homes, as originally designed, would have had three bedrooms along with a parlour and kitchen downstairs – quite comfortable for a family our size. But that was never the intention, and not how most people on the street lived. My parents rented the house and sub-let the top section to the Kennedys, a family with a noisy squad of kids who provided Mum with plenty to complain about. Later on, the Kennedys moved out and we took over the top section of the house, presumably to avoid having another set of noisy tenants above us. The downstairs flat was let to an elderly English woman called Mrs Jones and her dog, Lassie. She lived alone, though she was visited regularly by her middle-aged son. Sometimes he would stay over, and one day Mrs Jones found him dead. He had hanged himself.

My memories of the upstairs flat are the most vivid. There was a large bedroom at the front that had been partitioned into two rooms: one for my parents and the other for my sister and I. Behind that was the room where we did everything else: cooking, eating, sitting, bathing, watching television. My parents would sit on a stiff armchair and do piece work for extra money. They would assemble biro pens or insert transistors into Stylophones, a kind of small electronic organ that was advertised on the telly by Rolf Harris. Further back, on the return landing, was another room that I don't recall us using. It stored massive bags of unassembled pens, though in one corner my father had built a small partition room that housed a chemical toilet. This was to save us having to trek out to the back garden to use the flush toilet we shared with Mrs Jones. But I avoided using the chemical loo whenever I could. The room was too dark and it smelled funny.

There was no bathroom. We had a pink plastic bath that was gradually filled with water from a boiled kettle.

I would play mostly in the bedroom. I had two Action Men, a Major Matt Mason, a teddy bear and an old doll of Helen's, all of which lived in a house I constructed from cardboard and yards of sellotape my father would bring me home from work. My favourite telly programme was *Lost in Space*, and I hoped that when I grew up everyone would own lasers and jet cars and be able to visit the moon any time they wanted. When Mum wasn't looking, I'd slide around on the lino floor of the kitchen, pretending I could fly. I would ascend to one of the cupboards under the sink and sneak out the biscuits needed to sustain my super powers: custard creams.

We went to Saint Joseph's Primary School on Goodson Road, a worn Victorian building with Harry Potter-esque turrets, dark wood floors and brick walls glazed the colour of the Atlantic. Many of the kids in my class lived nearby. Kevin Edmunds (Irish father, English mother) lived two doors up. On the other side were the Harmons, also Irish, who had only one child, Adrian. Not a cool kid. My best friend lived two streets away, on Franklyn Road. His name was also Sean, though his surname is lost to me now. There were other children we knew from playing on the street. George and Maria White lived in an upstairs flat like us, but it was much more modern. The Whites had a washing machine and Maria got to wash her hair *every day*. Helen had a friend named Susan Smith who was Catholic but went to mass only at Easter and Christmas. Her father was English, her mother Cypriot. Due to their à la carte Catholicism, our mother didn't approve of the Smiths.

And there was a man who lived opposite, whose name we also can't remember now. But he was Irish and we would regularly see him at mass in Our Lady of Willesden Church, which, confusingly, was located in Harlesden. He would light lots of candles, but never took communion. The story was that his wife had divorced him, and because of this the man assumed he was excommunicated, but had always been too scared to ask a priest.

We were aware of who was Irish and who was not, but only just, and only because our mother felt the need to point it out. We were young and had no concept of nationality and all the historical weight that went with it. At the time, 'Irish' seemed more a statement of worth. 'Irish' was good, others not so much.

But we knew we were different, which was something else she constantly reminded us of. We lived in a huge, callous city, where the vast majority of people were not like us; so different, in fact, that they were to be suspected. And the main way that difference manifested itself was not through nationality, but religion. Or to put it another way, being Irish and Catholic seemed largely the same thing. Ireland was the home of Catholicism, and it was the best thing to be. Below that were Irish Catholics who didn't fulfil their responsibilities through omissions such as not going to mass every Sunday, and below that, a tiny sub-group that our mother referred to as 'good-living Protestants'. At the time I didn't know there was such a thing as English Catholics, or Irish Protestants. I thought they were all mutually exclusive. Helen can remember, when we moved to Ireland, being shocked that the Irish weren't quite as devout as how our mother had presented them.

The reminders of our Catholicism were constant, like a protection from the primeval tangle around us. We went to a school where morning prayers were part of the routine; at night we would be corralled into saying a decade of the rosary; and every Sunday we would make our way to Our Lady of Willesden Church, an enormous Romanesque hall with vaulted ceilings and back-stiffening chairs. I would be dressed in short pants and a blazer, while Helen had to endure itchy Crimplene suits, a mantilla to cover her head, or worse, a hat that would be secured by way of a pin plunged into her skull.

The church was so large that it seemed as if every Irish Catholic in London went there. The mass was gruellingly long and broken up only by the walk to take communion.

Helen could do this before I could, and I was nakedly jealous of her for it. Making my confirmation after that seemed eons away, and extravagantly grown up.

Expressions of Irishness were less regular, and felt more like an allegiance, like supporting a football team. There were records that would be played: *Seven Drunken Nights* by the Dubliners or Val Doonican, who also had his own television show, where he would inoffensively croon and wear jaunty jumpers. Helen did Irish dancing.

But the main expression was in our holidays. Despite all the financial stringency, every year we trekked to Ireland for two weeks. At a time when the package holiday was still a rarity, going to *another country* every year did mark us out as different. It was fantastically exciting, almost exotic, and even today the metallic sounds and smells of the car ferry make me slightly giddy.

The journey, however, was tortuous. A six-hour drive to Holyhead, a three-hour crossing, followed by an equally long drive to wherever we had rented a holiday home in the west of Ireland: Westport or Swinford or Galway. The location would be chosen on the basis that it was close enough to Castlebar, where our cousins, the Dunfords, lived. The dates would be chosen so that my father could attend the Galway Races with my Uncle Alfie, something they did together for decades after.

Alfie was the golden child of my mother's family, being the eldest, the only boy and the one who went to study medicine in UCD. But due to a chronic lung condition, he never completed his degree and so returned to Killala to live with my grandmother and, after that, with his sister Kathleen and her husband, Tom Foy (for some reason never made clear to me, he was always referred to as Tom Foy, even by Kathleen). Because he was in receipt of a disability pension, Alfie never worked, but he did invest considerable energy into studying horses. He had a room filled with dusty towers of newspaper clippings and he had a professorial grasp of the form and history of various horses, jockeys and trainers. But how often, or how much, he gambled was not known. He would deflect all such enquiries with a bluff jauntiness. For years I would ask how he did at the Galway Races, and I always got the same answer. He would hold up one finger, meaning one pound, but wouldn't say whether he had won the pound or lost it.

My middle name is Francis, after my father, who everyone called Frank. Alfie, in a gently teasing way, would always call me *John Francis*, as if to remind us both of where I was born and where my father came from. On holidays I would proclaim to my aunts and uncles and relatives that I was Irish – because they always asked, and I always wanted to please them. I have wondered since if Alfie was telling me no, you're not – and you don't have to be.

But this is retrospective speculation. On another occasion, while on a visit to Killala, Alfie brought myself, my sister and one or two cousins to see a cow being slaughtered. It took place in a shed not too far from my grandmother's house. I was about six at the time and had no idea what something like that might involve: that a gun-like implement would be put to the animal's head, shooting through its skull, and that the animal would squeal and stagger while pints of brown blood gushed from the hole. A man tried to control the dying cow and collect the blood in a basin.

I don't know how long this went on for. It seemed like hours, at least for however long I remained there. I ran back to the house, wondering what was wrong with me that I couldn't witness what the others seemed to be able to watch with casual interest, though later on, Helen admitted that she, too, was horrified. When they returned, Alfie, as jaunty as ever, asked, *What happened to you?* I made some excuse. Perhaps he was making a point by bringing us there, or perhaps it never occurred to him that all that death and blood might be difficult for a six-year-old to take. But it was the first time that it occurred to me that Ireland was different to where I lived, that being Irish might involve more than just saying it.

Our visits to Killala were usually brief – day trips for the most part. It was always quiet and smelled of turf. We'd be allowed to go down the street to small, pungent shops that sold red lemonade and crisps that were much cheaper than in England. Invariably it would be an old woman behind the counter who wouldn't be able to understand our accents.

Most of my holiday memories, though, are of being in Castlebar with our cousins, the Dunfords. Although we came from one of the biggest cities in the world, it was the Dunfords who seemed more sophisticated. They were confident and funny and played music and seemed to have a more complete sense of who they were and where they came from. I can't remember them displaying any interest in what our life in London was like. Castlebar was all they seemed to need. They belonged to it and it to them. Although I wasn't quite aware of the feeling at the time, I think I envied this.

The only variation to our trips to Ireland was when my grandmother died. At enormous expense, we flew from

Heathrow (the first time for all of us to be on a plane), hired a car at Dublin and drove down, a trip punctuated by stopping to let Helen throw up; she'd rather enjoyed the plane food.

Granny was laid out in the front room, though at the time I don't think it registered with me that this was an actual dead person. It looked too fake, like a porcelain copy. And anyway, I had barely known this woman (my grandfather died before I was born). Like much of the Irishness in our life, she was distant: the sender of five-pound notes on our birthdays, and copies of the *Western People*. Because of this distance, because of the eternal summer in which it seemed to exist, Ireland had formed a mythical status in my mind. It was a place where nobody worked or went to school, where everybody was pleased to see us and keen to give us money for sweets.

At some point my father changed jobs and began working for Roussel Laboratories, a pharmaceutical company that produced, among other things, the drug Mandrax, which for a time was popular on the disco scene as Mandies or disco biscuits. The job involved a promotion and the possibility of more advancement, and it would eventually take us out of London. One Christmas we attended the Roussel panto, where various men my father worked with sang songs and dressed in grass skirts. One of the performers called out, *Who's from London?*

I put up my hand, only to have it whisked down by my mother. *No you're not*, she hissed. *You're Irish.* She said it as if this had always been self-evident, as if what I had just done was a profound act of betrayal. It was the first time I think I realised that I couldn't be Irish *and* from London. I had to choose.

In the 1960s there was some concern that England was becoming bottom-heavy with industry and jobs – that everything was coalescing around London and the South East. The Expanded Towns Act gave tax breaks and other encouragements to companies to relocate a bit further north in what became known as 'overspill towns', one of which was Swindon in Wiltshire.

There wasn't a precise moment when we were told of the move. It was, rather, something that was a long time coming and well prepared for. Roussel organised coach tours to see the town, the schools, what places we might live in. Swindon was an old railway hub in some decline, but thanks to the Expanded Towns Act, it exploded in size. During the years we lived there, there was constant building.

The day we left, we were given money to get sweets at the corner shop. I bought a plastic tank with chewing gum inside. Some of my friends called around to say goodbye, and they briefly ran after the car as we drove away. I waved goodbye to them out the back window of our dark green Anglia and it occurred to me that I would never see these people again. I never did. I was nine.

There was, however, much to distract me. For the first few months we lived in a council house, something our mother disapproved of in principle but was prepared to tolerate because it was a *house*. Number 1 Taplow Walk provided Helen and I with our own rooms and an indoor bathroom (we were warned *never* to mention our previous bathing arrangements to anyone in Swindon). There was even a hatch that could be used for passing food from the kitchen to the dining area. We never used it as we always ate in the kitchen. But when my mother wasn't looking, I enjoyed climbing through it.

We made friends on the very first day. The Bonds next door had a son and daughter roughly our ages. And they were Irish too, though they were *Dublin Jackeens*, a sub-category of Irish that our mother found suspect.

Yet it seemed as if Swindon was already fulfilling its promise. We lived just across the road from a shopping centre where we would go for sweets or to pick up the *Advert*, as everyone referred to the *Swindon Advertiser*. I remember the day decimalisation came to Britain, and running over with my old shillings and pence to swap them for the shiny, gold-coloured coins.

In those days, parents didn't agonise so much, or at all, over every psychological bump their kids might hit. But if Molly and Frank Moncrieff had wondered about how we had adjusted to our new situation, they would have been pleased. We both settled quickly in our new schools. Helen's was Saint Joseph's Secondary and mine was Holy Family Primary, a school less than 10 years old and located on the same street as the equally new Holy Family Church, where we went to mass.

Within a few months we had moved again, this time to a house we owned. Covingham was a massive estate bolted onto the east side of Swindon, consisting of a central park and dozens of streets emanating from it like bicycle spokes. The streets were wider than usual, designed more for kids to play on than cars to drive on. All were in the style of the time, though the design varied depending on what street you lived on. Some were dormer bungalows, others more conventional semi-detached or detached. Although my parents coveted a dormer, we ended up in a three-bed semi-d. Number 5,

Finchdale. All the streets were named after birds: Heronscroft, Wrenswood.

Many parts of it, including the plot across the street, were still being built, but that just added to the sparkling newness of the place. In London our life had been consumptive and claustrophobic. We followed the same dusty path to school every day, walked on ancient stained pavements, on treeless streets filled with the sounds of rattling traffic and the mustard smell of exhaust fumes. In the evenings we squeezed into our tiny, dim flat. A trip to a park, or even the sight of grass, was a rarity. Cows and horses were exotic creatures. And now we were in a house, a *whole house*, more than twice the size of where we had lived before, but with acres of green to play on and building sites in which to construct adventures and sustain injuries. There was a reservoir within walking distance where we made rafts out of pallets and polystyrene. There was a VG shop on the other side of the park where we would buy crisps every Thursday, and swings we could go to *any time we liked*. It was brighter, cleaner and safer than anything we had known before. Even our mother seemed to relax in terms of marshalling us. Previously, going out the front door required permission and detailed explanations of wheres and whens. Now she was surprised to find us at home.

This was the future I'd dreamed about, finally arrived. Men had landed on the moon and every week on the telly *Tomorrow's World* told us about all sorts of breathtaking gizmos we'd be using in the next few years. By the time I'd grown up, there *would* be flying cars and holidays on Mars. In Swindon it seemed as if it was all going to come true. Nearly everything around us seemed crisp, full-colour and newly made.

Helen's school, Saint Joseph's, was the only Catholic secondary school in the town. It was a massive education factory. Even then there were more than 1,000 students between the lower and upper schools. Many were not Catholic, or only nominally so, and those who were came from a wide range of backgrounds: English, Polish, Italian, even Scottish. They had surnames like Perrigo, Harris, Porter, Donnachie and Chambers (which we were told was a Mayo name and worthy of approval).

Holy Family, perhaps because it was smaller, was more homogenous and seemed dominated by Irish. Even the teachers were Irish. Mister Nolan had a bass voice like Eamonn Andrews and used to tip out his blackboard duster on my head. Virtually all my friends were Irish too. The Mullane brothers, whose parents were friends with the singer Gilbert O'Sullivan (who had grown up in Swindon). Gavin Doyle, with a father from Graiguenamanagh in Kilkenny and a mother with a sardonic Northern Irish lilt. Such was the torrent of boys scrambling through her house that sometimes I'd knock on their back door and hear back, *Oh, go away.*

There was, almost instantly, a community we belonged to, much of it orbiting around Holy Family Church and Covingham. For a year or so I was an altar boy, which I was never particularly good at. I could never remember when to ring the bell or bring the wine to the altar. And I couldn't stop sniggering, or farting to make whoever was beside me snigger too. Still, I did get to hold the communion paten during midnight mass when the aforementioned Gilbert O'Sullivan was there. This remained my claim to fame for many years afterwards.

Helen joined the Legion of Mary, and as a 13-year-old girl, she and another would be dispatched to visit elderly Catholics who lived around Covingham. As they were representing the Legion, they were invariably let in. Sometimes the person would be pleased to see them. At other times the recipient of their kindness would remain largely silent, waiting for them to leave.

Dad got involved with fundraising for the church and before long had made friends, mostly with people who lived nearby. We went to their houses and they came to ours. In London this had never happened. In London we had been made to feel that we were different – refugees in an alien city. In Swindon this sense almost completely dissipated. I remember some kid in Covingham once asking me, *Are you Catholic? What's that like?* But this sticks in my memory because of its rarity. We lived in a place where it seemed many of our neighbours went to the same school and church and originated from the same country. Our parents' friends were all Irish: the Kellys and the Finnegans. Yet whenever they used the word *home* they didn't mean Swindon or the estate or their house. *Home* always meant Ireland.

Home was the place where we all went on holidays or where we would speculate about one day going back to live. It was slightly idealised, a fantasy place, and all the more unobtainable for that. In retrospect, perhaps many of them enjoyed the idea of Ireland – of returning there – more than the reality.

But for my mother it was still different. Swindon may have been better than London, but it still wasn't what she wanted. Even when she seemed to be enjoying living there, it was grudgingly so. It was still a foreign country, a place of heathens and subtle anti-Irishness. Owning a house, becoming lower middle class, was beside the point. As Helen put it, we were still the Israelites, bereft until we could return to the Promised Land.

So Dad started applying for jobs, filling out forms and travelling for interviews. When he finally landed one and the news was announced to their Irish friends in Swindon, the reaction was oddly muted, as if by acting on an aspiration they had all voiced, my parents were judging them, pointing out their hypocrisy. Some were more frank. I can remember one finally blurting out to my father, *You'll never stick it back home* (then, and for the rest of his life, people would regularly forget that he was Scottish, not Irish).

In the months before the move, I was aware of a tension between our family's long-held ambition and my contentment with life in Swindon. The parents of my friends would continually ask, *How do you feel about moving to Ireland?* They asked so often that I came up with a stock response: that I was happy. But I wished I could bring Covingham with me. I was 12. I didn't want to let anyone down.

For Helen, by then 15, it was far more difficult. She cried when they told us and made it plain that she didn't want to go.

My father travelled over before we did. He had to start work, leaving our mother to arrange the move and the house sale. She didn't cope with it well. It was a time of snapping and shouting, where we seemed to be betraying her with even the smallest complaint. We missed the balancing presence of our father. We'd go down to a phone box in the park and conduct brief conversations over a scratchy phone line, where it sounded like the person on the other end wasn't Dad at all.

Mum would complain to him about how much she had to do while we'd relay our nuggets of childish news. He'd give enthusiastic responses, though at times the line was so bad I suspect he couldn't hear what we were saying. Helen and I would argue over who got to speak with him for the longest.

His absence provided a distraction, in an odd way. Being so keen to see him again blunted the edge of finality about the move. And unlike London, we both made all sorts of unrealisable plans to see our friends again. They'd be coming over to Ireland for their holidays. It was possible. They'd already asked their parents, who'd said *We'll see.* But of course it never happened.

Sleepy-headed from an overnight crossing, we ate rashers in the Busárus bus station. Dublin seemed a bit glum in the dirty morning light, but at least familiar in the way all cities are. Rather than nag our mother about where he was, she kept saying it to us: *Where's your father? Where's your father?* As if we knew something she didn't, as if he had simply forgotten to collect us or had decided not to bother.

He arrived, harassed by the bad traffic, just as we finished eating. Helen and I wrapped ourselves around him.

For about a month we lived in a damp grey house on a field close to the village of Ahascragh, and after that we moved to another rented house close to the train station in Ballinasloe. And just as in Swindon, we were lucky. I made friends with boys on the street even before I started school, and who, I'm pleased to say, remain my friends today. We played football and other games on the plot of grass beside Tom's house across the street from mine or wandered along the railway line. For the four of us – me, Tom, Ciaran and Brendan – the railway line was a playground and also a sort of living symbol – of other places, where we hoped something better was happening.

For the first few weeks, even months, life in Ballinasloe felt as it did when we were on holiday. We bought a house in a new development. It was not dissimilar to one we had lived in in Swindon. Starting school was an adventure, and at first, probably because of the novelty I provided, it gave me a lot of positive attention. It was only gradually that my differences to everyone else became apparent. In class I knew nothing about Irish history. I had an exemption from studying Irish and so was consigned to sit at the back while the others recited guttural-sounding phrases. I wasn't sporty, so football or hurling were not options. The kids around me seemed rougher and louder than what I was used to. They openly smoked cigarettes and were familiar with social codes and cues of which I had no knowledge. I kept getting things wrong, but without knowing in what way I had made a mistake.

Perhaps two months after starting school, one of the other boys called me a Brit bastard – a declaration that, in my naive state, I found completely shocking. We had come back. We were the returning Israelites. But we weren't. We were blow-ins, a phrase I'd never heard before.

In writing about Ireland and the Irish, the word *contradiction* will probably come up more than any other. So here we go. So much of the story of Ireland is about the pain of emigration, of families and communities hollowed out. Yet the returning emigrant and their family can find it difficult, particularly so if they are not originally from that specific village or townland. The Irish are, in my experience, capable of being gregarious and ostensibly friendly, but also quite closed. When a new person arrives in the community, the level of acceptance they receive is in proportion to their own history and connection with that area. The less connection there is, the less acceptance they get, from a returning local at one end of the scale to a 'plastic Paddy' at the other.

I don't want to overstate this. It's a very subtle process and probably unconscious. It's rarely intended to be cruel. But it is there. Only since I've begun writing this have I noticed that over the years I have made a habit of asking immigrants similar to myself how they found settling in Ireland, and invariably they reported a difficulty fitting in and an initial surprise that the difficulty was there at all. Some shrugged and got on with it. Others found it deeply hurtful. They had spent years feeling like a foreigner in England, only to return and be made to feel like a foreigner here too.

Incidentally, this is not a phenomenon unique to rural Ireland. For some years I lived in Howth, where it's possible to be considered a blow-in if your ancestors haven't been there for at least 500 years.

So we mourn the Irish emigrant, but we are slightly uncomfortable when they come back, particularly if they don't sound the same as us. The Irish-American essayist John Jeremiah Sullivan has written about arriving for the first time in Ireland, his mind sizzling with ideas about roots, heritage and blood wisdom, only to have them all quickly smacked out of him. 'Nobody cared about "Irish-American"; nobody wanted to hear about it. Were you born here? Then you're not Irish.'

I was lucky in Ballinasloe in that I already had three good friends, yet unlucky in that, for reasons now lost to me, I was sent to the technical school rather than Garbally College, where my friends went. Whatever the reason, we had certainly misread the opaque social structure of the town. Largely due to our mother's doggedness, we were now firmly middle class. The arc of Helen's life and mine would now reasonably expect university, or a good job in the bank or the civil service. The tech was the working-class school, with a much lower set of expectations for its students – a job in one of the factories (in the early 1970s, Ballinasloe was relatively prosperous) or a return to the farm. For many of my classmates, this intention was baldly stated. At certain times of the year, the boys who lived on farms wouldn't turn up for a stretch of several weeks and wouldn't even pretend to make an effort to learn. Some of them could barely read, and many of the teachers were far too unmotivated to do anything about it.

I wasn't consciously aware of these differences, but I was aware that I had to make some sort of effort to fit in. So I lost my accent, and within the space of a few months I sounded as Ballinasloe as anyone else.

No one seemed to notice this transformation, or at least no one ever mentioned it to me. In later years, after I'd left the town and moved to Dublin – when I'd developed more of a sense of myself – my accent flattened out. Now I probably sound like I'm from the east of the country: a middle-class Dub – appropriately, a West Brit. But sometimes that old accent comes back. When I meet up with my old friends or even on the radio when I interview people from outside the capital, the old syntax and burr returns. *Ingine* for engine. *Fadder* for father. The ghosts of an old insecurity.

Helen was also lucky in that she made enduring friendships, though she thinks the two years she spent in school in

Ballinasloe were marked by a degree of rebellion. She thinks her accent (which she didn't work to lose) gave her a slightly exotic gleam among her friends. She can remember being told that she was okay for a Brit. We arrived when she was 15. By 17 she had completed the Leaving Cert and landed the good job in the bank. Financially independent, she was able to make some trips back to Swindon, but even that gap of two years had changed things. It wasn't the same; her life and friends were in Ireland now. After moving around Ireland a bit with the bank, she now lives in Ballinasloe with her family. But she says she didn't come to regard it as home until many years later, when she was married and they bought their own house.

After the Inter Cert I moved school to Garbally College. I had settled into life in Ballinasloe, though never completely. Even among my friends there was a shared history before my arrival that I wasn't a part of. There were people and places and events that I didn't know. That feeling never completely left.

Our mother got Helen and I Irish passports soon after we arrived, perhaps fearing that we might rebel and claim British citizenship. Yet despite bringing the Israelites back to the Promised Land, she still didn't seem happy. She would complain about Ballinasloe and, sometimes, about Ireland, though she would bridle at any suggestion that life in England was better. Perhaps she couldn't shake off the decades of wanting to come back, of wanting to be elsewhere. She had resisted ever accepting England as her home and now couldn't change that habit in Ireland.

Of course, it was a different country to the one she remembered. It always is. It was messy and loud and disorganised. The television was full of political rows, moaning about recession, arguing over sex. It wasn't pious and pure, as she remembered. That place had gone, if it had ever existed.

I didn't consider this at the time. I took her discontent as a function of being Irish – that to be Irish meant to complain about the place; to find it entertaining but also infuriating; to say *that's so Irish* as an example of laziness and illogicality and hypocrisy.

Years later, when she was dying, a nurse suggested that perhaps she had been suffering from depression for years. And perhaps that's true. There was certainly a constant restiveness. In my Leaving Cert year my parents moved again, this time to Castlebar, where they consolidated their middle-class status by building a four-bedroom detached home.

It was similarly unfulfilling, particularly so as Helen and I had now left home. They were alone in a large, empty and pointless house.

Eventually they returned to Ballinasloe, where at least they got to see their grandchildren grow up. They are both now buried in Creagh Cemetery, just as you enter the town.

After the Leaving Cert, I took off for college in Dublin. I didn't return that much. There was something about the anonymity of the city, the dust, the pavements, the traffic noise, that made me feel more at home. Even the briefest of visits back to Ballinasloe left me feeling trapped, suddenly panicked that I'd never get out.

I did the journalism course in what was then the College of Commerce in Rathmines, part of which involved a week-long trip to London to visit newspaper offices. The red pillar-boxes, the rubbery smell of the Tube – it was all so strange and familiar at the same time, like a half-remembered dream. I visited Cobbold Road. The house, as such things always are, was much smaller than I remembered. I bumped into Kevin Edmunds's mother, who seemed faintly amused that I would come back there just to look at a house. *All changed now*, she said. *Now it's all Indians, sitting out on the pavement. Didn't you get tall? And that accent.*

At the weekend I got on a train for Swindon. I had directions to some social club that took me hours to find. But as I came in the door, unsure if it was the right place, Gavin Doyle grabbed me in a bear hug. At first I wasn't even sure if it was him. I had forgotten so much.

The rest of that night was a drunken blur, filled with a rotation of people, many of whom I didn't remember or recognise, who asked after Helen and my parents, who marvelled at the fact that I wasn't a little boy any more.

And nearly all of them said it: *You sound so Irish.* I was a foreigner there, too.

It was after that visit that I started to put a lot of earnest, young-man thought into the question of my nationality. It was obviously too late to go back to being English. And I didn't want to anyway. So I simply chose to be Irish. Nationality is a cultural construct, so I constructed my own. I'm not Irish in the same way as many other people are. I wasn't born and bred in the same place. But I do belong to the long emigrant tradition of this country that spread Irishness all over the world, for it to mingle with all the other ways of being.

When people in Ireland ask me, I usually say I'm from Ballinasloe. Yet I spent barely six years of my life there. It avoids having to go through the longer tale, and Irish people, so taken with the notion of place, so keen to fit you into the jigsaw pattern of Ireland, find it unsatisfying when you start to explain that you are from several places – or none of them.

I'm from the Fifth Province – the place Mary Robinson identified in her inaugural speech as president. She intended it as a way of thinking about a new pluralist Ireland, but also as a way of including the 70 million people around the world who claim Irish ancestry.

During the 1970s, more than 100,000 people returned to live in Ireland – the first time the country experienced more people coming in than leaving. Many of them were like my sister and me – the sons and daughters of emigrants, kids who were happy to return to the land of their parents, of their holidays, but who, perhaps after a while, began to feel, as Helen puts it, that they weren't quite one thing or the other.

If Helen thinks about it, which isn't very often, she'd say that she is English with Irish parents. That's not because she forgets where our father was originally from. Oddly, he turned out to be better at being Irish than our mother. More than once, people remarked – though never to her face – that our mother was quite English in her ways. Needless to say, she would have found such a remark devastating. When we first arrived in Ballinasloe, Helen identified herself as English, though over time this changed. Her original accent is all but gone, and if she's abroad she says she's Irish. Like me, she finds it easier to tell the simple story. Yet there are English components to her nature that she doesn't deny. She will queue and obey the law and pay her car tax. She wouldn't be able to sleep if she didn't. I find that I'm somewhat the same. I like things to be ordered.

I have a fetish for stationary, something that I feel is peculiarly English.

Yet I couldn't be anything else other than Irish.

That's my story, one that I suspect is not that unusual. It's not the defining story of my life, just one of them. But it is an example, perhaps, of what has been happening in Ireland for the last decade or so, because as I said at the beginning of this chapter, Ireland, and the definition of being Irish, is changing.

Not everyone will like this idea, but there is an historical inevitability about it. Cultures all over the world are adapting and evolving for the simple, unassailable reason that things change. They always do. We lost Irish as a daily working language more than a century ago, and now even our accent – once the most solid identifier of Irishness – is under threat. Thanks to globalisation, television and the online world, it's now not uncommon to hear teenagers in Roscommon speak like natives of Orange County.

So, like, does this totally dilute what being Irish is? Or, OMG, does it threaten to extinguish it altogether?

Actually, no. What's remarkable about humans is how we cling to identity, especially national identity. We have clung to Irishness – in fact, the idea of Irishness has grown stronger – *despite* repeated invasions, famines, emigration and an often-malfunctioning state.

What's tricky is when we attempt to define *exactly* what being Irish is or even what the component parts are. All the clichés don't really help. Brace yourself for this revelation, but pretty much every nation on earth likes to think of itself as friendly and literary and music-loving and fun. In fairness, we do drink a lot of tea. But Turkey and Morocco drink more.

Perhaps it's genetic. The traditional story is that we are a Celtic people, descended from the *Keltoi*, a rather kick-ass race who made even the ancient Greeks nervous and who settled in Ireland 2,000 to 3,000 years ago, wiping out the original inhabitants in the process. But apart from some similarities between old Irish art and that of the Celts, there's little evidence that the Celts came here at all.

A study undertaken by Trinity College in 2013 traced a particular gene in Irish men called Haplogroup 1. It's extremely common here – 78.1 per cent of Irish men have it. But it's not Celtic. Our closest genetic neighbours are in the Basque country, and one of the study's main findings was that our ancestors probably came from Spain and Portugal around 9,000 years ago at the end of the last ice age. They were the original inhabitants of this island. They built Newgrange.

So does that mean that Haplogroup 1 is the Irish gene? Well, yes and no. Because Connacht is on the western edge of Europe, it has had relatively few incursions from the outside, genetically speaking. People have surnames that date back over 1,000 years. In Connacht, Haplogroup 1 is found in a whopping 98.3 per cent of men.

But it diminishes the further east in Ireland you go, down to around 50 per cent in some parts, due to the fact that the then native Irish had more opportunities to get frisky with the visiting English Normans and Vikings. And the original carriers of Haplogroup 1 went to more places than Ireland. For a time it was the dominant gene in Britain – including England – and spread to many other parts of Europe, but was diluted over thousands of years through contact with other races. Yet it can still be found in Scandinavia and even North Africa.

So unless you want to argue that only people from Connacht are truly Irish, or that Ireland, all of Britain and large parts of Europe are in fact originally Irish, or that none of us are Irish, but in fact Spanish, genetics isn't that useful in definitively pinning Irishness down.

What about culture then? There is much we can point to as being uniquely Irish: the music, the literature, what we watch on television, the sports we follow. The difficulty comes with people who don't identify with much or any of these cultural artefacts, yet who still would regard themselves as Irish.

Take two imaginary women, both called Mary, both born in Ireland. Mary 1 lives in Connemara and speaks Irish as a first language. She plays the tin whistle at the weekends and is a member of a camogie team. She watches *The Late Late Show* and never misses the Rose of Tralee.

Mary 2 lives in Dublin. She speaks English and promptly forgot every bit of Irish she was taught in school. She has no great interest in sport but does go to spinning classes to keep fit. She likes French wine and European movies when they are on at the IFI. She rarely watches television, preferring Netflix or box sets. She likes American singer-songwriters and has never watched the Rose of Tralee. She'd regard it as naff and a bit embarrassing.

These women are both Irish citizens and neither would have it any other way, yet apart from geography and a passport, they have very little in common. They would have radically differing ideas of what being Irish involves, of what being Irish *means*.

What does it mean to be Irish is one of those calcified clichés we love to trot out in public debate. But is this even the right question? Does being Irish have any inherent meaning? Is it the same as asking what it means to be a printer cartridge or a biscuit? Does Irishness represent a set of values or at least a way of being? American-ness is commonly seen as valuing 'freedom' and personal advancement. The English are seen as a fair people.

The Irish? What are we?

As I've suggested already, all the traits we ascribe to ourselves as if we invented them can be found in most parts of the world. Genetically, we're Spanish/English/French/Nordic. There are elements of a unique Irish culture, but we are also part of the globalised drift where most cities are starting to look the same and popular culture here is almost identical to that in Wisconsin or Manchester.

Yet the idea of Irishness persists, in a we-know-it-when-we-see-it sort of way. There's *something* about Irish people, about the way our minds work.

So let's reframe the question. Not what is Irishness, but *what is Irish*? What is that mental state that gives us our national identity and what are its characteristics?

First a little bit of history. In her book *Ireland in the Medieval World*, the historian Edel Bhreathnach describes how from the sixth century onward, various historians began attempting to write the Irish origin legend.

Legend is the key word here, as before the sixth century there was little in the way of written records in Ireland. Not that these historians (most of whom were based in churches) were too bothered with accuracy. The intent was different. In writing the story of Ireland, they happily combined facts, myth, speculation, tradition and bits cribbed from the Bible, the aim being to big up the Irish as much as possible.

The accounts are many and various, but all were singular in their aim to present the Irish as descended from nobility, from the learned, from characters in the Old Testament and even from deities (interestingly, one of the most common legends is that the Irish are descended from the sons of Milesius – who came from Spain). As Oxford professor John Carey wrote of the *Lebar Gabála Érenn* (or *Book of Invasions*), it was 'a national myth which sought to put Ireland on the same footing as Israel or Rome'.

During the medieval period, Ireland was regarded by most of Europe as a rural backwater, yet the stories we told ourselves were quite different – that Ireland was the nexus of the world. Or as James Joyce put it in *Ulysses*, Ireland was an *omphalos*: the navel of the planet.

Perhaps this self-aggrandisement came from hubris or an inferiority complex. Either way, it bears a striking similarity to the national myths we indulge in today. We never miss an opportunity to tell ourselves we are great – or to tell others when we are abroad. Then, as now, we put considerable energy into 'claiming' people. When Gregory became Pope in 590 AD, Irish scholars wasted no time in stating that his people originally came from Kerry (Gregory was born in Rome).

Bhreathnach also cites the example of Columbanus, who spent much of his life travelling around Europe with no great desire to return to Ireland. Yet he spent most of that time establishing monasteries based on the Irish model, as he felt it was superior. Later in his career he became embroiled in a

row with some German bishops over the date of Easter. So
Columbanus wrote to the Pope (the Kerry man, Gregory) and
calmly informed him that the system for calculating the date
– which was widely accepted across the church – was wrong
because Irish philosophers and mathematicians thought so.

It was an astoundingly cocky claim to make, but there is
something very *Irish* in the way he made it. Columbanus
combined chutzpah wrapped in a self-deprecating charm:
traits that seem peculiarly Irish.

Just as it was 1,500 years ago, we are still a small, relatively
unimportant country, but one with a knack for getting
attention. Our media finds the Irish connection, relevant or
not, in pretty much every big foreign news story. We take
refuge in clichés (*punching above our weight; they love the Irish
in country x*) to reassure ourselves that we are making some
imprint on the world beyond our shores. This seems to be not
a tradition, but one of the myriad ways in which we express our
national personality. There's an Irish way of using language, of
reacting, conducting relationships, making jokes, arguing, of
being in the world.

All the factors discussed so far have contributed to this
personality, along with many others that are still contributing
to it. Because, like most people, our national character has
changed slightly with each new experience. We are not the
people we were 500 or even 50 years ago.

Personality types, be they individual or national, are
tricky to pin down. People act in different ways in different
situations. We can be changeable and inconsistent and
downright hypocritical. Indeed, any portrait of a personality
is meaningless without these contradictions, especially in the

case of Ireland. In the 2006 movie *The Departed*, which features Irish-American gangsters, Colin Sullivan (played by Matt Damon) declares, 'what Freud said about the Irish is: we're the only people who are impervious to psychoanalysis.' Like any other race, we like to mine the myth of our exceptionalism, even if that comes from being contrary and exasperating and impossible to fully understand. It sounds like it *should* be true. Except it's not. Freud never said it, and the writer of the film, William Monahan, admits he got the line from the internet. It's not impossible to analyse the way Irish people think. Just really, really difficult. As the cultural theorist Terry Eagleton says, the Irish want to be different while also wanting to be the same as everyone else.

The idea of an Irish way of thinking has been the subject of quite a bit of academic debate. In the 1980s the Irish philosopher Richard Kearney published a book called *The Irish Mind: Exploring Intellectual Traditions*. Here's what he thinks:

Could it be that the Irish mind, in its various expressions, often flew in the face of such logocentrism by showing that meaning is not only determined by a logic that centralises and censors, but also by a logic that disseminates: a structured dispersal exploring what is *other*, what is irreducibly diverse? In contra distinction to the orthodox dualist logic of either/or, the Irish Mind may be seen to favour a more didactical knowledge of both/and, an intellectual ability to hold the traditional oppositions of classical reason together in creative confluence.

Academic debate isn't very exciting.

He's taking the scenic route to get to the point, but what Kearney seems to be saying is that classic European thought is based on logic, meaning that if you make a statement that contains a contradiction, then that statement must be flawed. The Irish Mind, however, doesn't operate that way. It can consider two ideas that contradict each other and find them both to be true, and this is a source of creative power.

Psychologists have devised different models to describe personality types, and each has varying degrees of usefulness depending on what you're looking for. But for a general look at personality, the most commonly used model is known as the Big Five Personality Traits.

So this is what I'm going to do. This book will unfold in five sections, each devoted to one of these aspects of personality. I'll make a stab at ascertaining if we have a lot of each particular trait, a little or, more confusingly, a lot and a little at the same time. The five traits are:

- Extraversion
- Agreeableness
- Conscientiousness
- Neuroticism
- Openness

Clearly, I'm not a psychologist. But like most people, I dabble. This is simply a framework I've pilfered to build a book around. I certainly won't be sticking within the strict psychological definitions. Nonetheless, I hope it makes some sense.

If you're Irish, you've probably already started to make judgements about how we fare in each category. As you read on, you will no doubt disagree, perhaps vehemently, with some of the admittedly subjective conclusions I will come to. But that's Irish too. It's our intellectual ability to hold the traditional oppositions of classical reason together in creative confluence.

It's the only country in the world where we can disagree and both be right.

Chapter 2

The Myopia of Pints: Are We Extravert?

In my twenties I went back to live in London. It wasn't a call back to my roots or even economic desperation. At the time I was a freelance journalist (though often 'freelance' was a nice term for unemployed). It was more the case that Dublin was dank and dreary. It was littered with deserted shop fronts and crumbling buildings. It was boring and without promise. And I needed an adventure.

It was also easy. Thanks to Michael O'Leary, the so-called Ryanair generation was able to move without having to feel like it was banishment. I moved to London and was back visiting within a few weeks. This was a new, middle-class form of emigration where most of the people travelling had degrees and aspirations. Kilburn was still there, a place of maudlin music and grim bachelors. But it was a grotesque novelty, filled with the dismal ghosts of the 1950s. In 1980s Ireland, you couldn't find anywhere like it any more.

And it was shrinking. Many of the older Irish had already moved away to the outer suburbs and become absorbed into the greater London population, to be replaced by creeping gentrification. Kilburn was being rebranded as West Hampstead.

I visited it once, just to have a look. Afterwards I walked up to Cricklewood to see where I used to live and to take a picture of the Galtymore Dance Hall, where my parents, and just about every other Irish person in 1950s London, used to go dancing. It's closed now.

When I told my parents that I was moving to London, I had expected my mother to be furious. All that nagging and saving to get us back to Ireland. But she wasn't. She simply said *oh no* in a fatalistic tone, as if she had been trying to save me from the life she'd had, but all along she'd known she would fail.

Camden Town was still something of an Irish haunt, but it had a younger and more punkish air. I'd drink in the Liberties Bar (now replaced by a gastro pub), where, over a span of about five years, I always managed to just miss seeing Shane MacGowan.

But I wasn't there that much. Spending time in the company of other Irish people was not a necessity. This was a more confident generation, and being in London in the late 1980s seemed to give a further boost to that confidence. These were the days before the peace process, yet apart from ignorance about the difference between Northern Ireland and the Republic or the occasional Irish joke (usually told to me as if I'd enjoy this kind of thing), not once did I ever experience any anti-Irish feeling that I was aware of. This was due, I think, to the class difference. I was a middle-class person in a middle-class job. Such was the cultural sensitivity, there was a near-embarrassment about being English. People who (to my ear) had English accents would insist they were Scottish or Welsh and try to conspire with me in gossip about what the English are like.

Being Irish had a cachet that I hadn't been aware of before. All too often, as soon as I opened my mouth, people would start to make a series of positive assumptions about me: that I would be charming and funny; that I would have a creative, almost mystical aspect to my nature; that they would like me.

At times, being Irish can feel like a burden. We are complex and coded. We can be weighed down by resentment and truculence and prejudice. For many of the Irish people I knew then, moving away was a mild revolutionary act – a rejection of an Ireland still mired in depressing arguments about divorce and sexual morality and the necessity of hating the Brits.

It felt easier to be Irish in London than it did in Ireland. This was Irishness with all the bad bits rinsed out. It was possible to be any version of Irish you wanted: atheist Irish, tattooed Irish, gay Irish. For me, it was especially liberating. For the first time, I didn't feel any sense of ambivalence about where I was from. Everyone I met regarded me as Irish, and I embraced my new, clearly defined identity with perhaps a little too much enthusiasm. I found myself describing, ad nauseum, Ireland as a work in progress – a country that would, in the not-too-distant future, become the tolerant, fair, peaceful society I hoped it would. But while I did that, I heard myself utter nationalistic sentiments I had never had before or since. I once described Northern Ireland to an English colleague as the 'unliberated territories', and while I never expressed support for the IRA, I did let people infer that I knew quite a lot about that sort of thing. I would occasionally use the few phrases in Irish I knew, and for the first time insisted upon the use of a *fada* in my byline (I worked for a trade magazine for the TV industry called *Broadcast*). But I had them place it over the wrong letter.

It was ridiculous. While I didn't act this way around any Irish people I knew – where invariably the conversation would turn to complaining about the Ireland we had left – I couldn't resist presenting this vivid new version of my nationality to others, something which seemed to intrigue English people. Or at least it seemed that way at the time. The English, after all, are extraordinarily polite.

I was trading on a perception that does seem to be true: everyone loves the Irish. Certainly I've experienced it in pretty much every country I've been to, and usually not on the basis of some *Darby O'Gill* stereotype. Invariably, they've met an Irish person before, found them to be delightful and assume you will be the same.

It's not particularly scientific, but it is indicative. Type 'everyone hates the Irish' into Google and you get 298,000 hits – and many of those entries are about what Irish people hate about themselves. Type 'everyone loves the Irish' and you get 5,100,000 hits, much of that from foreigners (particularly Americans) detailing how much they learned and gained in terms of personal growth from visiting here.

There's good reason for them to have had that reaction. Just as it was easier to achieve a better version of Irishness in London, we can do it when dealing with tourists in our own country too. Almost as if we are all part of an unspoken collective PR effort, we'll ask tourists if they need directions. We'll ask them where they are from and make some effort to make a connection with that place. We'll share some small details about ourselves and make sure to depart their company while they still want more. We have the uncanny gift of making foreigners fall in love with us in five minutes.

It's when it goes past five minutes that things become a little more complex. No, a *lot* more complex. But we'll get to that.

So are we an extravert nation?

Clearly, we are. Clearly, to use the cliché we love so much, the Irish are great *craic*. That spelling, by the way, is one that gives some academics grinding pains of irritation. It was originally spelled *crack* but at some point was Gaelicised, probably in the 1960s, and made popular in the following decade by the broadcaster Seán Bán Breathnach, who would promise *beidh ceol, caint agus craic againn* for his RTÉ TV show *SBB ina Shuí*. The word is actually Middle English in origin, when it was spelled *crak*. It travelled north into Scotland, then across the sea into Ulster and made its way south only in the middle of the last century. Nonetheless, you can find hundreds of websites and books telling you that the word comes from the Irish language and is barely translatable into English.

But in fairness, the provenance of the term isn't that important. What's significant is how we stole it, made it our own and beamed it back into the world. It's a one-word branding exercise, suggesting the idea of an ancient people with their own unique way of tackling the mysteries of existence – who dredge every last morsel of joy and creativity from life. It makes us sound fun, but also a bit mystical, like we've figured out something profound. And if you come to visit, you might too.

Many, perhaps most, visitors arrive here and leave with that impression still intact. Because when they walk around the streets or shyly enter the pubs, they do see us singing, laughing, talking. Always talking. Oscar Wilde said the Irish are 'the greatest talkers since the ancient Greeks', and by this he didn't mean the *amount* we speak but the *way* we do it.

It's a rare thing for an Irish person to speak in facts. For the most part, we tell stories. *Any stories?* is still a common conversation opener, as is its urban counterpart, *What's the story?* Someone relates an event from their life, or someone else's, and then another person in the group continues with their own tale that may or may not be relevant to the first one. And so on.

We don't like to call it this, but a lot of these stories are in fact gossip. Visitors might like to think that we spend much of our time arguing about politics and religion or discussing books, but in fact our natural urge is to strenuously veer away from such subjects. All too often, they might lead to bad feeling and kill off the *craic* we are attempting to generate. It's much safer, and much more fun, to talk about other people – people we know, or people we know who know the person being gossiped about.

The gossip can be malicious, tragic, heroic, simply funny or somehow instructional (there is a peculiar Irish habit of ending stories with the words 'so now …', leaving the listeners to infer that some moral lesson is embedded within what they have just heard, even if there isn't). But because Ireland is still such a small and (relatively) unpopulated country, the stories nearly always take a particular form. For the tale to have credibility, the teller has to claim to know the person who witnessed the event.

Some examples.

There's a story about a well-to-do woman who orders a dress for some society event. The dress has to be altered in a hurry and then delivered to her home. The delivery woman arrives at the house but gets no answer when she rings the front doorbell. Because of the urgency of the situation, she proceeds to the back of the house, where she witnesses the woman having sex with an Irish celebrity to whom she is not married. The delivery woman then leaves the dress and flees.

I've been told this story by people who know the delivery woman from the dress shop (the celebrity later comes to the shop and asks her to be discreet). I've also been told the story by people who met the taxi driver who delivered the dress (he was given €500 to keep quiet – unsuccessfully, it would seem).

The Irish classicist John Pentland Mahaffy once claimed that he was only ever beaten once as a child – for telling the truth.

Another utterly bogus story concerned the singer Ronan Keating, one so pervasive he felt the need to appear on *The Late Late Show* to deny it. I have heard it in so many iterations that it morphed into a tale about the broadcaster Ronan Collins. And some years ago, people I have known for decades met a woman at a dinner party who told them that I was gay, that I have a long-term boyfriend and that she was a close personal friend of mine. I have no idea how widespread this story became, as it has only been repeated back to me on that one occasion.

Despite their love of gossip, Irish people also have an instinctive discretion. If Ireland is small enough to create a personal link to the subject of any story, it's also small enough to trace the story back to its originator. This discretion, though, is also historical. As Terry Eagleton says, 'the Irish used speech as a way of hiding their true thoughts from their rulers'. Novels like *Castle Rackrent* gave us the stock Irish character who flatters his landlord so extravagantly that it comes across as endearingly stupid. But in fact it's a device to distract the landlord from what the cunning tenant is really up to. We even have a word for it: to *plámás*. And yes, you guessed it, it's not an Irish word either. It comes from the Norman term *blancmanger*, which means to be bullshitted by an Irish person. More or less.

Loving gossip is not unique to Ireland, but what is unique is that need to present a personal connection to the story and the fact that telling stories seems to be more socially prized than listening to them. Here comes another great Irish cliché: we are a nation of storytellers.

Yes, there is a tradition of storytelling in this country dating all the way back to the ancient *seanchaí*. Much of our traditional music is story based, usually involving dozens of verses and some morbid tale of death or injustice or heartbreak. Or all three. But pretty much every country in the world has similar traditions. Some Irish people, like the writer Colm Tóibín, baulk at the Irish-are-natural-storytellers stereotype because it implicitly undermines people like him who put a great deal of work into constructing stories.

For the non-professional, storytelling – or gossiping – isn't about relaying information anyway. It's about *having the craic*. If the philosopher Marshall McLuhan were sitting in an Irish pub, he would once again conclude that the medium is indeed the message, the medium in this case being the person who is telling the story. The person who tells the most stories in the most entertaining way is deemed to be the most *craic*, which in Irish social situations is considered high status.

So when that foreign tourist goes into an Irish pub and witnesses what seems to be a relaxed situation populated by smiling, chatting people, what's going on is in fact far more ritualised. There are unspoken rules about what should and should not be spoken about – rules that are also interlinked with how we consume alcohol (we'll come back to the alcohol question later). That tourist has probably already met individual Irish people presenting the best version of themselves to her. In the pub, she is witnessing Irish people *doing it to each other.*

Nowadays, though, we get to do this not just in the pub. We do it on social media, to which we seem to have an astonishing addiction. More than half of us have a Facebook account, and according to one survey we use it more often than any other country in the English-speaking world. But there are also rules operating here in terms of how we use it. Just like in most other countries, many of us use it to post links to articles that are illuminating or inspirational or feature pictures of kittens playing badminton, but again there is this phenomenon of Irish people presenting the most positive version of their own lives.

You've probably seen it yourself. One of your Facebook friends is out at some restaurant or bar with some other friends who are all tagged in the post, often along with a picture to demonstrate just how much fun they are having. In fairness, Facebook is constructed in such a way that 'negative' posts are gently discouraged. You can hardly announce that you're missing a dead relative and expect others to 'like' it. The point is that we *get* Facebook because we were all in the self-promotion business long before the arrival of the digital era.

But being Irish, we find it a bit irksome when we see others doing this. A survey by Eircom found that one-third of respondents were annoyed by others constantly posting photos.

Twitter, though, is more complex. Again, we are enthusiastic about it. We send out about one million tweets a day, and per capita, we are the tenth highest users in the world. However, those figures do beg a little analysis. That's one million tweets over a 24-hour period and it includes retweets and multiple tweets from the same account, which is most users. At its busiest, there are not even 60,000 people using Twitter in Ireland at any given time. During the slower periods, a hashtag with as few as 160 mentions can get it trending. I point this out because there's often an implicit and explicit assumption that Twitter somehow reflects public opinion in this country. It doesn't. It reflects Twitter, which tends to be younger, leftish leaning and, when it comes to politics, a bit more angry.

Like any other form of social media, Twitter is used for a variety of purposes: to share jokes and videos, play hashtag games (my radio show is responsible for one on Fridays), make stupid jokes that can get you into trouble (I've done that) and of course to sell you stuff.

But in my experience at least, Twitter has become the forum in which a lot of the anger caused by the collapse of the economy has expressed itself. Since 2008, the mainstream media has been waiting for mass protests and civil disobedience, and when it never came we wondered why the Irish were so docile in the face of grinding austerity.

Instead of protesting, some Irish people choose to give out on Twitter. All sorts of campaigns have been launched and have died there, along with individuals who use their accounts as a form of agitprop – posting links to articles and challenging politicians and members of the mainstream media. It's difficult to tell how many politicians engage with this sort of thing, though my guess is not many. A lot of them don't operate their own accounts anyway, and for those who do, the exchanges usually devolve into name calling and cheap point scoring. Dan Boyle, a former Green Party senator, is the only politician I know of who regularly engages in the proscribed kind of debate Twitter offers, and from the slagging matches I've witnessed, you'd wonder why he bothers (indeed, it was reported in 2010 that some of his Green Party colleagues weren't too enamoured of his Twitter activities).

So why does he bother? Perhaps he enjoys the debates, such as they are. But there is also the fact that, occasionally, Twitter can be a lethal political weapon. In 2010 the then Minister for Defence Willie O'Dea had to endure a no confidence vote after it emerged that he had sworn an inaccurate affidavit in defence of a defamation action against him. O'Dea survived the vote and seemed safe, but then Boyle tweeted, 'I don't have confidence in him. His situation is compromised. Probably a few chapters in this story yet.' The tweet enabled the mainstream media to chase the story again, and O'Dea resigned 24 hours later.

In the same year, when Taoiseach Brian Cowen gave an interview to *Morning Ireland* on Radio 1 and sounded decidedly ropey, the Fine Gael TD Simon Coveney tweeted, 'God, what an uninspiring interview by Taoiseach this morning. He sounded half way between drunk and hungover and totally disinterested.'

Yes, the word he should have used was *uninterested*. Nonetheless, the tweet gave the mainstream media the chance to ask all sorts of questions about the Taoiseach's social life that they wouldn't normally ask.

Yet apart from that, Twitter is a terrible place to conduct a political discussion. With just 140 characters in which to express an idea, the posts are often little more than superficial declarations or abuse, and sometimes they are lies. Politics and the organisation of a society are complicated, messy, never perfect and usually nuanced. Twitter is the opposite of that.

But I suspect that's the attraction. To put it at its unkindest, it is the perfect place for armchair revolutionaries and conspiracy theorists to make bold, unproven assertions about the world or people of whom they disapprove. What's also notable about the angry Irish political tweeters is the high proportion who operate their accounts using a fake name, often something portentous like A New Dawn or Rescue the Republic (I made up those particular names). There's even a web term for it: *performance piety*, a form of display behaviour aimed at demonstrating how committed/angry/compassionate these individuals are.

All of this suits the Irish cast of mind. We'll come back to this later on in the book, but the Irish have been politically lazy. We engage with the people we elect only if we want something personally, and we talk about them in the most facile way: they're all stupid or in it only for themselves. Irish politics may annoy us, but we rarely *do* anything about it. The Greeks and the French have a tradition of street protest. In the Nordic countries, voters demand (and get) high levels of transparency and accountability. In Switzerland, direct democracy is practised. In Ireland, we ring Joe Duffy. Or give out on Twitter in the hope that somebody else will actually leave their house and do something about it.

In fairness, this may be changing. There was a massive anti-water charges protest in late 2014. When the government announced a fixed, less-than-expected charge, subsequent protests weren't as big. But they have been big enough to signal that perhaps significant change is finally taking place in Irish politics. But we'll deal with that later on in this book.

Our habit of docility isn't entirely our fault. We have been cowed by various autocrats, both political and religious, for centuries. Despite the clichés, we are not a confrontational people. Our long tradition of revolution is actually a long tradition of revolution carried out by a tiny minority while the rest of us put up with things as they were. The Fighting Irish is an American football team and nothing more. And there's a massive strain of fatalism in the Irish psyche. As the author Niall Williams put it, 'The History of Ireland in two words: Ah well.'

We prefer to fight our battles in a far more coded way or, just as often, not at all. Thus, Twitter, in the Irish political sense, is a form of therapy masquerading as political activism. It provides the illusion that ordinary citizens can vent their anger to those in power and, as a result, effect change. It's simple, quick, often anonymous and no doubt makes some people feel better. But, alas, it changes nothing.

We are not a confrontational people for another reason too: because there's not that many of us and it's a small country. It's always wiser to maintain friendly relations – or the appearance of friendly relations – with as many people as possible, and for that to work effectively there is a coded system of discretion. Yes, we love to gossip, but only in strictly defined circumstances. Visit New York and you'll regularly hear Americans having loud and personal conversations without much regard as to who can hear them. An Irish person would *never* do that, and we are slightly appalled by people who do. The travel company Expedia carried out a poll in 2014 among 25 nationalities and asked various questions about mobile phone use, including, 'Do you find the use of speaker phones in public places offensive?' The nationality who most objected to it were the Irish.

We may have used language as a way of hiding our true thoughts from our rulers, but we still do the same thing to each other. There are all sorts of quaint and sometimes clichéd examples (*I'm only staying for one*) of how we can say one thing but mean the opposite. For example, we seem to have an inability to say *goodbye*, as if the word itself is offensive. Instead we resort to synonyms such as *I'll let you go*, which implies that your interlocutor and not you is the person who wishes to end the conversation, or that they are performing a kindness by talking to someone like yourself – a prime example of *plámás*. On the phone, we sign off with a bizarre over-use of the word *byebyebyebye*, as if this somehow dilutes the offense it may be causing.

Leaving an Irish house after a visit can be a long and sometimes frustrating affair. Once the visitor has announced their intention to go, everyone stands, but the conversation can continue as if they hadn't actually said it. They may then move into the hallway, where there's another pause for conversation, and a third pause outside the front door of the house. Sometimes the process of leaving can take longer than the actual visit, and again this is a ritual – a way of demonstrating that the hosts were not in any way remiss in their hospitality and that the visitor is regretful about having to leave at all. It is somewhat courtly, and rather sweet.

However, there is no greater example of the coded nature of Hiberno-English (the dialect we speak) than our use of the word *grand*. It can mean everything and absolutely nothing. Probably the most common greeting in Ireland is *How are you?* (or *Howareya?*), to which there is a *pro forma* response of *I'm grand*. It's not really a question or an answer, merely a way of opening conversation. However, depending on the tone of voice, *I'm grand* can mean *I really am grand* or *I'm not that great but coping with a difficult set of circumstances*. Similarly, describing something as grand, say, a film, can range from meaning it was pretty good to just about tolerable.

No, you're grand is often used in situations of mild conflict. For instance, if an Irish person complains about their food in a restaurant (still a rarity), they will invariably go on to apologise about making the complaint, to which the server may respond *No, you're grand*. Again, depending on the tone, this can range in meaning from *You were perfectly within your rights to make that complaint and I'm glad you did*, all the way up to *You're annoying and I want to spit in your food*. We are using language not to give offense, but at the same time we are highly attuned to the subtle messages embedded within the words.

At the risk of pointing out the obvious, these are generalised observations to which there will be many exceptions. This book will be full of them. You may be an Irish person who never speaks in this way. But that's okay; you're grand.

To the visitor, though, who is usually tone deaf to all this, it sounds like we are permanently jolly and upbeat. All of which brings us back to the tourist entering the pub and witnessing *craic* unfold in real time. She will assume it's all spontaneous and natural while not knowing the coded way in which we communicate. She will also assume that the Irish are really friendly.

Here's Terry Eagleton again: 'Irish culture … is devious, complex and multi-layered. It's very much an in-group culture, full of codes, hints and signals which an outsider has to decipher. Beneath the appearance of openness, Irish society is a fairly guarded place, a lot less accessible than it seems.'

So, the better you know the signals, the better your chances of fitting in, even of making friends. In the previous chapter I touched on the difficulties faced by the children of returned migrants. But it seems as if their parents – even if they are originally from the area they have settled in – face similar problems.

Over the years a number of academic studies have been done on this. One carried out in the late 1970s on returned migrants to the west of Ireland reported, among other difficulties, an inability to develop a proper social life; a study carried out in the 1990s on returned migrants to Achill Island cited 'unfriendly locals' as a problem; while a study carried out in 2007 cited a recurring theme of 'not quite belonging'.

In fairness, the discomfort of returning migrants can be put down to a number of factors. Having lived, perhaps, in a metropolitan area, it will always be a culture shock to return to a small place in the west of Ireland. The place won't be the same, and neither will the returning migrant. All the studies found that the longer the person had been away, the more difficulty there was in readjusting. However, they also found that the dissatisfaction levels declined over a period of years. The community started to accept them, and more importantly, they began to remember the social codes.

But what do you do if you never knew the social codes in the first place? Is it even possible to learn what the rest of us unconsciously absorbed?

Non-Irish migrants come here for a variety of reasons. During the boom years many came from Poland and central Europe with the hope of getting a job. A bit like Irish immigrants in London during the 1980s, they were usually young and had a ready-made community of other people in the same situation as themselves. Many, if not most, had no intention of establishing a long-term presence here and so were not particularly exercised about integrating into the communities they lived in.

However, many more did come here with the hope of establishing a life. Despite all the migration from around Europe during the boom, the largest migrant group here is the British, and they came because they either wanted to settle here or they had married an Irish person.

There are many expat discussion forums on the web, and they are very revealing. Time and again there is a shock at the difficulty of making friends in Ireland – a difficulty they clearly hadn't expected, and one they feel they can talk about only in the relative anonymity of the web. They might not understand all the social codes, but they know enough to realise that Irish people like to think of themselves as friendly, as the friendliest nation on earth. They'd be offended if they were told otherwise.

But don't get the wrong impression. There aren't thousands of immigrants bitching about us on the internet. In fact, what's surprising is the generosity of the tone. There's a familiar pattern. They go out of their way to state how much they love Ireland, they list off what they like about the place and about the people – the sense of fun, the way a stranger will help you. Yet they are baffled and disappointed that the ostensible friendliness they encounter all the time never translates into anything more durable.

An article published in the *Irish independent* in 2002 crystallised many of these experiences. Ho Wei Sim, a Malaysian woman then living in the west of Ireland, wrote that when people would ask how she found settling in Ireland, she would actually try to answer the question, but soon learned that what her questioners were looking for were a few bland but positive-sounding sentiments about the country.

'When we first arrived,' she wrote, 'everyone seemed delightfully friendly. We'd have lots of fun going to the pub, have many easy, even intimate conversations with people whom we had just met. They would ask you all about your life, ask very personal questions about things you wouldn't even tell your mother. You'd feel you made a connection, possibly even a great friend. And then all of a sudden it would stop.'

Over time she found herself in a social Groundhog Day loop. She would get to a certain level with people but never any further. She would find herself having the same conversation with the same people, and learned that what was expected from her was to be funny, be entertaining – have the *craic*. If someone expressed an opinion she disagreed with, it was best to say nothing. 'You simply learn to withdraw, to keep a distance; just like an Irish person would.'

Just like all the other expats, Ho Wei Sim believes the Irish are warm and welcoming. 'But it's a perceived warmth that can be misleading … it doesn't necessarily mean anything and that can be quite hurtful.

'They'd almost cut off their arm if they thought you needed it. But at the same time they don't invest in you and wouldn't care if they never saw you again.'

Multiple times, she wrote, she had conversations with other foreigners in Ireland who had had similar experiences, all of whom were surprised to learn that the Irish were in fact far more reserved than it first appeared. Once, shockingly for her, even an Irish person said it.

She believes the reserve comes from something we've touched on already: the small size of the country and the fact that Ireland, as a largely homogenous place (until recently anyway), has felt no great need to welcome in strangers.

But what she and a large number of the contributors to the discussion forums also identified was the role of alcohol as a sort of social and psychological safety valve.

'I think a lot of Irish people need alcohol in order to let go of the reserve, to loosen the tongue, to speak more frankly. Otherwise, people are too careful about what they say ... [the next day] there's always the excuse, it was the drink talking.'

In that observation she's right and she's wrong. Yes, we do need alcohol to get over our reserve, but we rarely say *It was the drink talking* the next day. We don't have to. Not asking about last night's conversation is also part of the code. The ritualised way we communicate with each other is inextricably bound up with the ritualised way we consume alcohol.

But before we get to that, a brief diversion. All this talk might leave you with the impression that Ireland is full of closed, soulless communities spurning outsiders. At the height of the boom there certainly was a perception that this was the kind of Ireland we were creating. Young couples, desperate to get on the property treadmill, would buy an over-priced house on some ghastly half-finished estate that could be two hours' drive from where they worked. They'd leave at six in the morning and not get back until after eight. They'd never meet the neighbours and at the weekend spend whatever time they had with their kids, who were already screwed up from having to spend 12 hours a day in childcare.

These estates would be bolted onto the side of a small village, yet they would never merge into one community. The young couple would be a ghostly presence there, until all the driving, the social isolation and lack of sleep forced them to emigrate or split up.

However, there's no great evidence of this sort of alienation. Indeed, in 2010 a group of sociologists published a book called *Suburban Affiliations*, a study of four commuter-belt areas around Dublin (which included Mullingar – that's how insane the boom was). Out of the hundreds of interviews they conducted, they found that a majority of respondents felt an attachment to the place they lived. They also found, on average, that each person had five or six other people on whom they could call for help or support, be it neighbours or family members.

But the authors were careful in their use of language. They wrote that these communities were sustained by 'loose but meaningful affiliations between residents' and even introduced their own pointy-headed term to describe it: *communality*, which they defined as 'affiliations that are neither entirely superficial nor deeply intimate'. In other words, friendly but not friends. Your neighbour will mind your kids for a bit or put out your bins or feed your goldfish, but she won't tell you how she's feeling.

It's the way we do things, and it's not all bad. It shows that even when various social and economic forces threatened to transform us into a colder society, we still managed to create communities.

But back to drink. Oh, we love a drink. We are champion drinkers. And the figures are disquieting. But first, some drops of comfort. The World Health Organization provides the technical definitions here, and for the WHO, 'binge drinking' consists of six or more units of alcohol in one sitting. Or three pints. To consume three pints over the course of an evening would hardly seem to be the stuff of waking up in your front garden. So keep that in mind when you read that, according to 2013 figures, 75 per cent of all alcohol consumed in Ireland is as part of a 'binge', that one in five Irish drinkers engages in a 'binge' at least once a week and that 31 per cent of us do it once a month.

Three pints a month. Big deal.

More difficult to dismiss, though, is the increase in our drinking. It's been steadily increasing since the 1960s. Between 1980 and 2010 it went up by 24 per cent, while in the rest of Europe it *decreased* by 15 per cent.

It gets even worse when we compare ourselves to other countries. In 2013 we came second out of 194 nations in our rate of alcohol consumption (Austria won). We may complain that the definition of binge drinking is a bit wimpy or that there are a number of ways of calculating consumption, but the inescapable fact is that we do drink more than pretty much anyone else. And it's not doing us a lot of good. Even as far back as 1999, it was estimated that the annual bill caused by harm from drink was £1.7 billion. And yes, that's in your old-fashioned Irish punts.

All these figures take into account another oddity of our boozing: 19 per cent of Irish adults *don't drink at all.* Perversely (or perhaps not), we have one of the highest teetotal rates in Europe. In a country where part of our national brand is pub culture, there's another culture that's almost completely invisible.

There is much public hand wringing about the problem. There's scarcely a politician, churchman or medic who hasn't expressed concern about how much we knock back, and in the media shock-horror exposés about our boozing pop up at predetermined times of the year. Saint Patrick's Day is always reliable, as is the night the Junior Cert results are announced. It's all too easy to park a hack and a snappy outside some nightclub. Inevitably, a paralytic teenager will appear.

The causes and therefore the solution to the problem vary. It's below-cost selling by supermarkets or it's Celtic Tiger indulgence (the number of off-licenses in Ireland trebled during the first seven years of this century). It's the introduction of wine culture, where middle-class people lure themselves into believing that knocking back a bucket of Shiraz while sitting in front of the telly isn't really *drinking*.

Much of the commentary is predicated on the idea that drinking to excess is a *recent* problem with the Irish – that the amount young people drink now is far in excess of what it was back in our day. Just a few pints. Bit of a singsong. (*A few pints* or *the odd pint* or *go for a pint* – more examples of our cunning use of Hiberno-English. The number of pints is never specified, but the language always implies that it isn't many, that it's totally benign.)

It is a fact that Irish people drank less in the past, if only for the pretty obvious reason that in the past, Irish people had less money to buy alcohol. But the *amount* isn't of primary importance here. What's more important is *how* we drink – what the *purpose* of our drinking is.

'Drunkenness had become widespread, and was the curse of all classes in Ireland.' So said the *Catholic Encyclopaedia* in 1838. In the first decade of the 20th century, the average number of arrests for drunkenness in Ireland was over 75,000 a year. The English traveller Fynes Moryson, who in 1617 published a Europe-wide travelogue called *An Itinerary*, specifically mentions how the Irish like to get drunk. In the last two centuries in particular, there have been periods of concern about our drinking, followed by mass movements (usually led by the church) to get us to give it up.

Now, the cliché of the drunken Paddy – in London, Boston or Ireland – is one that has been used to portray the Irish as feckless, self-destructive, stupid – somewhat less than human. But that doesn't take away from the reality that we have a complex and often problematic relationship with drink. And as far as it can be traced back, this seems to have been the case for a very, very long time.

But it's not just a matter of drinking until we fall down. As in other cultures, there are rituals and rules surrounding how and in what circumstances we imbibe. Drinking to excess is obviously not good for your physical well-being. It makes you fat and blotchy, and over time it can strain the liver to breaking point. The evidence suggests that some people are more susceptible to alcohol, for genetic or other reasons, and therefore to alcoholism.

However, the social circumstances also play a crucial part. In 1958, two American anthropologists published a paper on the drinking patterns of a Bolivian tribe called the Camba. Once a week, members of the tribe would sit in a circle and pass around a bottle of homemade hooch. They would do this all night. If anyone felt they had had enough, they could lie down, have a nap and resume drinking when they awoke. The anthropologists (who also took part) reported that people would get drunk, but never crazy drunk. There was no fighting or throwing up or crying. And the hooch was rocket fuel. When it was tested, it was found to be close to pure alcohol.

This weekly gathering was the only way the Camba drank. There was no evidence of some drinking more than others.

If we adopted this practice in Ireland or any other western country, some of the group would invariably become roaring alcoholics over time. But this didn't happen with the Camba. Somehow, their tribal culture blocked this.

Yes, I know. In the same way that you can always find a line in the Bible to prove just about anything, you can also always find some obscure tribe in a remote part of the world to do the same. What's important here is that the article brought the Center of Alcohol Studies at Yale University to suspect that perhaps something similar was happening on its own doorstep.

Yale is in the city of New Haven in Connecticut and had large immigrant populations, particularly Italians. Studies carried out on the Italian community had already found a keen love of alcohol. It wasn't uncommon for people to drink every day. It wasn't uncommon for them to drink with dinner, lunch and even breakfast. Yet a lot of them claimed they had rarely been drunk, and the pathologies normally associated with this level of consumption (which is a fancy way of saying the life-destroying features of alcoholism) were difficult to find.

Even more significant was the make-up of patients at the local Yale Alcoholism Treatment Center. There were 1,200 people being treated there for alcoholism, but only 40 were Italian. The other large immigrant group was represented by hundreds of patients: the Irish.

So the researchers had two large immigrant groups in New Haven, both members of the same religion, both fond of a drop. Yet one of the groups was hardly touched by alcoholism. This is why the Camba findings became important – it led them to suspect that culture was playing a part in New Haven too.

They did the obvious thing: they checked to see how consumption rates compared between the Italians and the Irish and found they were roughly the same. But the *way* the drink was consumed was distinctly different. The Italians would take wine virtually every day and always with a meal. In fact, the wine was regarded as *part* of the meal, not a thing in itself; it was food too.

The Irish, surprise surprise, drank hardly anything during the week but come the weekend would knock back the entire quota. They drank like Irish people. The way they were consuming it left them far more vulnerable to alcoholism. It still does.

So why do we drink this way? Well, we've got something in common with the Camba. That piece of research concluded that their drinking ritual was a way of bonding the community together. Because of poverty and long working days, they had no other affordable way of having a collective experience.

Our version of that is going to the pub – and buying drinks in a round. According to a study undertaken by Oxford academics in 2006, round buying is an important social ritual. Buying everyone in the group a drink displays esteem and affection, and because everyone takes their turn, it becomes a shared burden: paying for it, going to the bar, remembering everyone's order. In Irish pub culture, there is no graver sin than missing your round. Staying on your own, or worse still, not drinking at all, can be treated with outright suspicion.

Because here's the other important aspect of round buying: everyone is getting drunk at the same rate, and as that happens, the unspoken social rules are allowed to take hold.

Brief diversion while I explain the alcohol myopia theory. It says that alcohol does not have a hugely disinhibiting effect. Instead, it makes the drinker myopic to everything except their immediate surroundings. Pissed, and you don't think about the world outside the pub or yesterday when you swore you'd lay off the drink or tomorrow when you'll wake up with a hangover. It moves your immediate surroundings to the foreground, pretty much blocking out everything else. Thus, a group drinking in a round will all act the same, and in the Irish context this means bringing out that golden version of ourselves. It means being able to act and speak in a way outside of the constraints imposed by our daily lives. Indeed, while in that group, in that drunken state, those constraints no longer exist because we've forgotten all about them. For that night, we have become *different people.* Who wouldn't want that? It's why we are able to have intimate conversations with people we barely know or perhaps have never met before, but the next day we can go back to acting like it never happened.

The alcohol doesn't make this happen. More precisely, the alcohol facilitates what is a very well-established social ritual, one that can utterly baffle outsiders. In 1969, two American sociologists, Craig MacAndrew and Robert Edgerton, published a book with the fabulous title of *Drunken Comportment.* 'Persons learn about drunkenness what their societies import to them,' they wrote, 'and comporting themselves in consonance with these understandings, they become living confirmations of their society's teachings. Since societies, like individuals, get the sort of drunken comportment that they allow, they deserve what they get.'

Our society teaches us that drink and *craic* are inextricably linked, and that at a certain point in the night that can involve revealing ourselves to each other in a way we might not normally – to say what during daylight hours is left unsaid. But for this to function properly, the entire group must take part. There's something dangerous about it otherwise, which is why the non-drinker is treated if not with suspicion, then a certain amount of unease. If he says he won't have a drink, there's an assumption he's an alcoholic; if she says she won't have a drink, she's pregnant. Either way they have to explain why they aren't taking part, and many people find *I just don't drink* to be an unsatisfactory explanation.

For the sake of transparency, I do include myself in everything I'm writing here. I have been that drunken soldier. There is something delicious about ensconcing yourself in a pub and sealing off the outside world with all its irritations and impossibilities. I've often woken up with a hangover but also with a sense of lightness, as if I've unburdened myself. I have friends who I have known for years, who at a certain point in the night will always express the same unrealised dreams. I may do the same thing myself. I've been stupid. I've been fined for being 'drunk in a public place' (a McDonald's outlet – I was so plastered that I missed the door and fell through the window). Through one particularly difficult period of my life I drank every night for six months. Even now, when I've had a bad day or some upset, I'm still aware of that urge to reach for a bottle and make it temporarily go away.

So yes, we have a dangerous and unhealthy relationship with alcohol. But that's because we have an unhealthy relationship with each other – with ourselves. We flee from intimacy during the day, only to chase it at night.

This includes sexual intimacy too. In 2003, I presented a game show on RTÉ called *The House of Love* (it was dreadful, but that's another story). The basic idea was that a young couple would win a house, which was very much of the time. Even then, many people felt they had been priced out of the market.

As a result, the show received a massive number of applications. Initial auditions were held at various locations around the country. All the couples were asked a range of questions, including how they first met, and it was striking how, in the vast majority of cases, alcohol was a factor. There is an Irish culture of getting drunk and getting off with someone. It can be a one-off or it can lead to marriage. Either way, it's only slightly glib to speculate that if it were not for drink, the Irish might be extinct – or an endangered species, surviving only in zoos. Scientists would gingerly leave bottles of Jameson around the place in the hope it might encourage us to breed.

However, this is changing slightly. American-style dating has become more popular, and despite hundreds of years of Catholic puritanism, we seem to have turned out okay, sex-wise. But we'll come back to that later in the book.

You may be reading this and thinking, *But what about drugs? They are the real curse. Isn't that a problem too?* Well, yes, but given that this section is dealing with whether the Irish are extrovert or not, it's not strictly relevant. Our consumption of drugs is not guided by a set of social codes that go back hundreds of years. Our consumption of drugs is not linked to how we interact with each other as a society. In fact, the evidence would seem to suggest that we take drugs in pretty much the same way and for the same reasons as in most other western countries. This *is* interesting and relevant, as I'll explain in a little bit. Drug taking is a function of globalisation.

We were, pardon the pun, relatively late to the drugs party. They first arrived in the mid-1970s and even then not in any great quantity. It was students, mostly, smoking a bit of pot and making their own LSD. Drugs became a matter of public anxiety only when the heroin epidemic hit inner-city Dublin around 1979. This is where the globalisation bit comes in: because of the fall of the Shah in Iran and the Soviet invasion of Afghanistan, western Europe became awash with cheap smack. Just like in many other western countries, heroin became the drug of the poor and dispossessed, and in the Ireland of the time there were few places as wretched as inner-city Dublin. For people already in pain, heroin was the ultimate painkiller.

Since then, the use of all sorts of drugs has grown steadily in Ireland, and unsurprisingly – again, pardon the pun – it hit a high during the Celtic Tiger years, when we became one of the biggest users of cocaine in Europe. Despite the downturn, we still are, though contrary to what some newspapers would have you believe, the drugs problem in Ireland is not significantly worse than anywhere else in the European Union. Our recreational drug users are typical Europeans, typical citizens of the world, part of a (largely) youth global culture.

But drugs are only a tiny part of the globalisation process, which brings us back to where we started: the Irish as emigrants, projecting themselves out into the rest of the planet.

Historically, the reasons why we needed to move abroad have been various and unrelentingly miserable, at least in the way we tell the story to ourselves. Yet the very fact of it demonstrates how Ireland had been contributing to globalisation long before the term was ever coined. We moved in large numbers to every part of the English-speaking world. Consider this: in the 19th century, one million Irish people became US citizens – a bridge between the countries of such significance that the historian James Dunkerley claimed that in reality, Ireland is 'an American country located in the wrong continent'.

Despite our colonial past, and because of it, we've gone elsewhere to reinvent ourselves. Here's another contradiction: Irishness stands for roots and tradition, yet it also stands for exile and diffusion – a breaking away from those roots. At the same time, we are deeply parochial and expansively global. And although the reasons for Irish migration have been largely economic, they haven't been the *only* reasons. For generations, Irish people have been leaving Ireland because they wanted to. Even in the 1980s, I could have stayed. But the Ireland of the time seemed dreary and without much hope. Even at the height of the Celtic Tiger, when people were coming *here* to work, a study carried out by NUI Maynooth found that there were patterns of migration out of Ireland. Fleeing from home is part of being Irish.

We go away to reinvent ourselves, but we've tried it at home too. As the academic Declan Kiberd puts it, in the 1920s there was a 'reconstruction of the national identity, beginning from first principles all over again'. A new state, and a new Us. We were presented with a definition of our culture that was fixed and unchanging. Catholicism. Family. Friendliness. Self-sufficiency. Dancing at the crossroads – all that.

It couldn't work, either culturally or economically, so we began to change again. In the 1960s we started to look out at the world, particularly at the US, but in the 1970s we decided to define ourselves as European. It wasn't until the 1990s, though, that this internationalism really took hold. We had a bubbling economy and we finally had a decent football team (with the best fans in the world) and multiple Eurovision wins, which of course led to *Riverdance*. And then there was U2 and the Chieftains and Irish actors doing well in Hollywood and an Irish pub on every corner of every major city in the world.

Critics of globalisation say it's bland and corporate – that it contributes to an ongoing process of melting individual and distinctive cultures. It makes everywhere start to look and feel like everywhere else. The US is the largest contributor to this, but in Ireland we've done more than our fair share. When it comes to the globalisation business, we – to use that vile cliché – punch above our weight. The likes of U2 and *Riverdance* aren't *distinctly* Irish. They use a bit of Irish, mixed up with influences from a dozen other cultures and none, to make it easily digestible in Birr, Birmingham and Baltimore.

This is not necessarily a bad thing. It's the way the world is turning. But given that we in Ireland have engaged with this process so wholeheartedly, that our leaders and media regularly present this to us as a source of pride, it's bound to have an effect on the sort of people we will become.

Since the turn of the century, Ireland has regularly been cited as one of the most globalised countries in the world. This is largely an economic definition. There are more than 1,000 multinational companies operating here, which employ far in excess of 100,000 people. This means that we bob along on the tides of international commerce and hope all goes well.

The economic crash here was caused by the hubris and greed of our banks and the unimaginative timidity of our politicians. But a third factor was the international events over which we had no control. Yet despite that, in post-crash Ireland, there is not even the slightest effort to economically insulate ourselves from something similar happening in the future; rather, it's the reverse. The rush to attract foreign capital goes on apace. Rather than emigrate to reinvent ourselves, we can bring the foreigners here now – make Ireland the sort of global country that we'd much rather live in, filled with the sort of people we'd much rather be.

Added to that now is the genuflection before web commerce. The Dublin Web Summit – essentially a sales event for digital entrepreneurs – has quickly grown from kitchen sink beginnings to a hugely successful event, so much so that it's now de rigueur to devote acres and hours of media coverage to how wonderful it all is. It's doubtful that an international conference of, say, estate agents or gardeners, no matter how big, would attract such attention.

Now don't get me wrong. I'm not against foreign direct investment. I'm not against Ireland engaging with the outside world. I'm certainly not against the internet. But all this is having an effect, both economically and culturally. Digital entrepreneurism, with all its gobbledegook quasi-religious language, presents itself as far more than just a new method of selling stuff to people. It routinely claims to be *changing the world*, and to question such bombast leaves you open to the accusation of being a Luddite or, even worse, lacking *enthusiasm*.

Constant enthusiasm is an absolute requirement of the new digital global community. You see it in the entrepreneurs. You see it on Facebook. You see it on the gazillion YouTube channels that our kids are watching instead of television. And with all this comes a new set of cultural norms that affect real people in the real world. It's not simply Americanisation, either. These people can be from anywhere on the planet.

Obviously, the effect of this global culture can really be seen only among younger people at the moment, and even at that I suspect it's largely an urban phenomenon. I don't have any statistics or studies to back this up, but younger Irish people *seem* different – the way they speak; the requirement to sound positive; the lack of irony, of anger, of rebelliousness; the hugging; the routine tossing out of *love you* as a way to say goodbye. It's a way of being that seems crafted, almost a kind of spin, and it's something you can witness in pretty much every country in the western world and beyond. It's certainly not Irish in the way we've been describing it. Like *Riverdance* and any other globalised products, it's a sort of Irish-lite.

Again, this is just an observation on my part. It may have no long-lasting ramifications. It may simply be a youth fad that will peter out over time. Or it may be an international cultural shift of which Ireland is a part. It may eventually turn Irish people into bland automatons, or it may finally release us from the suffocating need to be careful about what public self we present to each other. Perhaps we won't need alcohol any more to achieve intimacy.

But what if this comes at the cost of what makes us distinctive? What if we continue to be an extrovert people, but no more or no less than anybody else?

Here's another contradiction, and one I find active within myself: the Irish are extrovert, but in an extremely controlled way. We are guarded and cute (in the Irish sense of that word), though we'd never admit it. We're not as friendly as we appear to be, even to each other. We rely unhealthily on alcohol to get us temporarily past our emotional constipation.

It's infuriating. It's juvenile. Yet when that tourist enters the pub and sees us having *craic*, she will smile, and not just because she's entertained. There will also be a sliver of envy, because she'll see us attaining a sort of wild state that few other nationalities can get back to. The others are too grown up now – too hidebound by their responsibilities and their own social codes.

There is something uniquely Irish and roughly beautiful in this. It would be a tragedy to lose it, because it would leave us somehow less than what we are today. But can you retain this without all the other weird, complicated, annoying stuff? Is it worth it?

Chapter 3

The Cóilean Deas Factor:
Are We Agreeable?

Every weekday morning I get the DART into town. I prefer it as I regard driving as an expensive waste of time. I can work on the DART. It's where I write my books. It's where I'm writing these words right now, having observed the proper protocols. I prefer to sit at the end of the train and when I enter the carriage I do a quick scan so I can avoid schoolchildren, Italian or Spanish teenagers or people with noisy headphones, all of whom, in various ways, produce a din that impedes my concentration. The rat-a-tat of the train lulls me into my work. It's the human sounds that distract me.

I also avoid junkies. No, it's not the politically correct term, but *drug user* is too broad in scope to indicate the people I mean. They are a cohort that dresses in a certain way (tracksuit, usually with the hood up), and who for some reason are always carrying a lighter that they flick nervously. They usually have bad skin and wear a peeved expression, as if they have just suffered some terrible injustice and would like to tell you all about it. Invariably, they get on one carriage, wait for the train to start moving and then stride urgently into another. They never close the door behind them. Ever. Why they do this, I have no idea. Why they happen to be on the DART at the same time as me every day is also a mystery. Perhaps they are travelling in to join the dealers and addicts who cluster around the Tara Street DART station. Perhaps they are heading into a clinic. I don't know. I don't really care. I just find them annoying.

Over the years, there have been one or two incidents. A couple of them once smoked heroin in the seat beside my then 10-year-old son and me. I said nothing. But I did on another occasion, when the acrid smell of it started to pillow around me. I stood and grandiosely strode off, declaring *I'm not going to inhale your heroin*, much to the shock of the grinning American tourists sitting behind me. The drug users told me to fuck off – repeatedly.

Junkies are loud. They have shouty conversations with each other, usually about how the social welfare and/or criminal justice systems are being so desperately unfair to them, and how they told him/her to fucking fucky fuck fuck. When alone, they have a tendency to corral others into conversation, even if the others don't want to. They say, *I don't want to bother you now*. But they still do.

Yes, I find them annoying. And while the reasons above are part of it, they are (to a degree) rationalisations for my annoyance. They don't get to the heart of it – to what I'm really feeling.

A few years back I was sitting in the DART at Howth station, waiting for it to move off. I had already started working on some book I was writing at the time, already despairing at some poorly constructed sentence I didn't know how to improve.

In walked a junkie. He carried a lit cigarette.

'Sorry, pal. Sorry. Sorry for disturbing you now. Sorry. Is this the next DART into town?'

Given that it was the *only* train in the station, and that the simple process of standing on the platform and looking *up* would have informed him that this train was about to depart in three minutes, the question seemed astoundingly pointless. I briefly considered a sarcastic answer, but instead I pointed at the cigarette.

'There's no smoking on the DART.'

I'd expected my snotty tone to produce a response in kind, or at the very least a surly withdrawal. But instead he looked startled, even alarmed, that he'd somehow disappointed me. He backed away, gushing apology until he was able to hold the lit cigarette outside the train with an extended arm.

'Sorry now. Sorry. Is this the next train? Sorry to disturb you.'

I gave a curt *yes* and went back to my work. He retreated outside with his fag.

The doors slid shut and the train jerked into motion, and it was only then that I noticed his presence. The carriage was completely empty, yet he had chosen to sit opposite me. Our knees were almost touching. I could hear him shifting about, coughing, muttering to himself, waiting for any acknowledgement from me. He was like a puppy, begging to be played with. I dipped my head a little lower and fought to concentrate.

'So ...'

I kept looking down.

'Are you a student?'

The words were delivered in such a tone of pale innocence, I almost smiled. I said *No* without looking up. He swept a knobbly hand at the edge of my field of vision. His fingers were burned yellow from smoking.

'Sorry to disturb you now. Sorry.'

I didn't reply, though I already knew that ignoring him wouldn't be enough. He seemed unable to help himself.

'So what do you do then?'

Concentration gone. My precious writing time ripped away from me. I snapped into my default smart-arse mode. I straightened up, looked him in the eye for a beat and turned the sarcasm up to eleven.

'I'm a professional gymnast.'

I am a bald, skinny, middle-aged man. Whatever amount of drugs would require you to mistake me for a student, it would take a vast multiple of that to believe that I am any sort of athlete.

He leaned back. His eyes widened with unabashed delight.

'*Reeeelly?* Like in the Olympics and that? Win a gold medal?'

'A silver,' I said.

I had been waiting for him to realise what I was doing – that I was taking the piss in revenge for him eating up my time with inane questions. But I failed to see what he was doing to me. Perhaps it was drugs (though he didn't seem out of it) or lack of experience or that he really was a deeply credulous person, but he seemed to believe me. Suddenly it was too late to go back on my story, not just because of my flowering embarrassment, but because the train had stopped a couple of times and other people were sitting around us. There was a woman with a buggy not even trying to hide the fact that she was eavesdropping. My new friend, being a junkie, was repeating everything I said to him at the top of his voice.

By the time we parted I had been forced to tell him all about my silver medal win, a back injury that had forced me to retire and my gym in which I now trained young Olympic hopefuls. As we parted, he gushed about his good fortune at having met me, about how he couldn't wait to tell his friends all about it.

But he didn't ask to shake my hand. Instead, he begged to be allowed to feel my bicep. I had to let him. I burned with shame for hours afterwards.

Perhaps I misjudged him. Perhaps he was a genius of irony and not the wide-eyed creature I assumed him to be. Or perhaps he still tells people about the day he met an Olympic medallist on the DART. I'll never know. As I left him, what I could be sure of was that I had been an utter dick. I hadn't been *agreeable*, and in the psychological sense this doesn't mean being great *craic* in the pub; we've covered that. It means to demonstrate pro-social behaviours such as trust and altruism. It means to be *kind*. I had met a man and instantly judged him on his clothes, the way he spoke and what I assumed were the circumstances of his life. I had been rude to him simply because he had spoken to me, and I continued to be rude while he continued to be nice to me. I hadn't seen a person, I'd seen a junkie. I operated as if I knew all about him when in fact I knew nothing. It is chastening to be confronted by your own bigotry.

There's probably a bit – or a lot – of bigot in all of us, though of course that's never an excuse. The point is to try to overcome it.

So as a society, how kind are we?

One straightforward way of rating this is how much we give to charity, and in this regard we do well. In 2011 the figure was €2.78 billion, and this was after a drop of 8 per cent brought on by the financial crash.

An organisation called Boardmatch Ireland tracks how much we donate, and found that the largest chunk of it goes to hospitals. A relatively small amount goes overseas. In the top 100 charities (based on how much money they raise), there are only nine overseas aid organisations. Collectively, they account for only 11 per cent of all charitable donations, which perhaps is good news if you're of a charity-should-stay-at-home mindset.

The news is even better when we compare ourselves to other countries. The World Giving Index reports that around 70 per cent of Irish people give money to charity, a result that puts us fifth in the World Giving Index Ranking. And if you must know, the top four are the US, Canada, Myanmar (huh?) and New Zealand.

The reasons for our generosity are pretty self-evident. We are an emigrant nation for whom poverty still lives in our folk memory. We are also a small country, which ensures that you or someone you know has been in need of a hospital, which probably explains why hospitals do so well in terms of donations.

The World Giving Index also asked how many Irish people volunteer their time. It came back with a result of 37 per cent, which again is excellent by international standards, and probably more significant. Throwing money, if you have it, into a basket is easy compared to giving a part of your day to the service of other people. However, what we don't know is what any of this volunteering entails, whether it was regular or people volunteering on a once-off basis, or if the figure is even that reliable.

Given the obvious huge economic and social benefits that volunteerism brings to society, it's surprising that successive governments have paid scant attention to it. In 2005, the pithily titled Joint Committee on Arts, Sport, Tourism, Community, Rural and Gaeltacht Affairs did produce a report, *Volunteers and Volunteering in Ireland*, though like many such efforts you could be forgiven for thinking that it was produced for the sake of it. In Irish politics, *producing a report* seems to be considered the same as *actually doing something*. As often as not, the committee doesn't even create the report itself. Once you've thumbed through the impressive cover page with the harp and the list of committee members, you discover that this document was put together by DKM Economic Consultants. All the committee did was come up with a list of bland recommendations, the first of which was that there should be more research. Your tax euros at work.

The report revealed, unsurprisingly, that volunteers tend to be happier as they have greater 'life satisfaction', that volunteerism is worth anything between €205 million and €475 million a year to the Irish economy and that the numbers regularly volunteering are, at best, unknown. More research is needed, apparently. A survey conducted by the National Economic and Social Forum in 2002 put the figure at just 17 per cent – one dramatically at variance with the World Giving Index figure. And when compared to similar surveys over the previous decade, that figure appears to be declining: it was around 38 per cent a decade beforehand.

Contributions from various voluntary groups (though, bizarrely, the GAA was not included) seemed to bear this out, with the vast majority reporting an increasing difficulty in attracting volunteers, particularly younger ones. This was 2005, in the midst of the boom, and the conclusion from most of them was that Irish society was cash rich (or so we thought at the time) but time poor. We were commuting, buying houses, having decking installed, picking up the kids from the childminder on the way back from work. It wasn't selfishness but the way our lives came to be structured. Being better off seemed to give us less time to give to each other.

Yet volunteerism then, and now, still goes on. In 2003, 30,000 people volunteered when the Special Olympics were staged in Ireland, and 177 towns around the country hosted national delegations. Athletes and their families stayed in the homes of ordinary Irish people. Away from the high-profile events, people help out with community groups and sports teams and drama clubs. Hundreds of thousands of them do it, but quietly, largely ignored by government and the media, so much so that we don't know how many there are or what sorts of things they are doing. The fact that they are ignored, that helping other people is not *championed*, does say something about the prevailing ethos in Irish society.

Yet, as we've already talked about, Irish people, individually or collectively, can be extraordinarily kind. It seems so ingrained in our national self-image that we are compelled to do it. We are friendly, albeit in a superficial way. Newcomers, both Irish and foreign, have found this to be the case. But what if those newcomers don't have the same skin colour as us?

Can it metastasize from bonhomie to actual unfriendliness? Or something even more disturbing?

What about racism?

You don't need me to tell you how the economic boom led to massive migration into this country, so massive that it has changed Ireland forever, and we are only just starting to realise how much. Around 4.6 million people live in the Republic of Ireland, and 600,000 (13 per cent) of those are what we like to call non-nationals (this figure was higher, but after the boom ended, many went home). Compare that to just before the outbreak of World War Two, when fewer than 3,000 foreigners (as we used to call them) lived here. By any measure, this is an extraordinary demographic and cultural change. We went from being a white, homogenous culture to a multicultural one in less than two decades.

Luckily, it all happened at a time when Ireland was starting to feel good about itself, and not just because of the money. Emigration and political violence, two elements that had scourged Ireland for hundreds of years, finally seemed to be coming to an end. We couldn't be told what to do by the Catholic Church any more, either. Ireland suddenly seemed cosmopolitan and alluring, so much so that, for the first time, outsiders wanted to live here. For a country often transfixed by what the rest of the world thinks of it, this was the ultimate compliment.

This more comfortable attitude was reflected in some studies during that period, particularly in relation to definitions of what it took to be Irish. The International Social Survey Programme found that the criteria for being Irish was becoming more relaxed, with fewer people citing birth in Ireland, having citizenship or even long-term residency as being important, which is just what you want when a major migration into the country is taking place.

There were some minor grumbles and some attempts to establish anti-immigration groups and parties, but none of them managed to achieve anything but miniscule amounts of support. It's arguable that most Irish people actually liked all the immigration. It made Ireland a more interesting, culturally rich place, and some of the nationalities that came, particularly the Poles, were welcomed as hard working and admirable. We developed a degree of sensitivity to issues surrounding racism. In 2011, the mayor of Naas, Darren Scully, had to resign following comments about the 'aggressive attitude' of 'black Africans'. When the then Fianna Fáil politician Mary O'Rourke used the phrase 'worked like a black' during a speech to party workers, she was promptly compelled to say sorry. In fairness, the words were more of a reflection on the generation she came from than any innate racism in her.

The most glaring reason for all this is pretty obvious. As a nation that suffered from emigration and all the prejudice and abuse that goes with that, we were hardly going to revisit those sins on others.

But let's not go completely nuts with self-congratulation. There *is* racism in Ireland. I occasionally hear it from listeners who wonder how I'd feel if a Pole took my job, and every year the Equality Authority deals with hundreds of cases of alleged racial discrimination. In 2006 there were 853 of them, and this number grew to 878 by 2009: not a dramatic rise given that by then the economic sky had fallen in – usually an opportunity for the Hard of Understanding to blame immigrants for Everything.

Similarly, the Gardaí record racially motivated incidents, and the figures from 2006 to 2010 show an actual *fall*. But this is where things become a bit hazy. According to a report released by the Integration Centre in 2013, racist incidents in Ireland are vastly under-reported. The Garda figure for 2012 was 98, but the Integration Centre claimed it was more like 240. The conclusion was that this was due to clunky Garda procedure as well as a reluctance to contact the guards – because of a belief that nothing would be done about it.

The various bodies concerned with the welfare of migrants report varying figures when it comes to racially motivated incidents, but all of them are considerably higher than the official statistics. They also indicate that a preponderance of them involve young men, often under 18. The Irish branch of the European Network Against Racism (ENAR) calls school holidays a 'peak period'.

ENAR Ireland also provides a breakdown of what sorts of incidents these are, with the largest three categories being 'shouting', 'harassment' and 'being treated unfairly or differently in public'. So, in fairness to the Gardaí, it must be said that some of these, while offensive and unpleasant, might be difficult to categorise as crimes.

None of it is acceptable, though. But that doesn't mean that Ireland *as a whole* is racist, just that, like most societies, we have racists among us. Based on the admittedly flawed Garda figures, Ireland compares favourably with many other parts of Europe. Officially, at least, Ireland is 27 times less racist than England and Wales. It's not a clear picture. There are inconsistencies, but if we were to make a semi-educated guess here, then for a country relatively new to immigration, we are doing pretty well.

But that's not the way we perceive it. A 2001 *Sunday Independent* survey found that 51 per cent of Irish people felt that the country is inherently racist, and 60 per cent in the 24 to 35 age group agreed that racism is an Irish trait.

There's no way of knowing what the respondents in this survey based these opinions on, so I'm going to guess: they based it on what they heard the occasional idiot spouting off about and items they may have seen in the media.

In my experience at least, the vast majority of the racist spouting centres on asylum seekers – that people arrive in this country, ask for help and are immediately given an apartment with sea views and the keys to a luxury family saloon. The reality is altogether more grim. They are packed into prison-like direct provision centres and given €19.10 a week to squander on things like baby food. (In June 2015, a Department of Justice working group recommended that this payment be doubled.) They can remain there for years while their application for help is being processed. Even if the spouters are aware of this truth, they are still more than happy to doubt their reasons for being here. And why wouldn't they? In the media, the term 'asylum seeker' rarely appears without words like 'bogus' or 'flood' attached to it. Almost universally, asylum seekers are presented as a *problem* – never, like the rest of the migrant population, as people attempting to make a new life for themselves and their families.

Here's some more truthiness. Out of the half a million migrants who have come to Ireland, asylum seekers constitute a few thousand a year, and the vast majority of those are (eventually) sent home again. Ireland has one of the highest refusal rates in Europe. We accept fewer than 10 per cent of those who apply, while the European average is 24 per cent.

So if you're a reasonable person and you've heard a couple of the spouters and read a few of the headlines, are you going to think Ireland is a racist country? Of course you are.

All right. So when it comes to outsiders who come to live here, we are, on balance, pretty agreeable.

Except when it comes to Muslims. I'm not saying that Ireland as a whole is anti-Muslim, but the racism they experience does seem to be more prevalent and of a distinctly different complexion to the taking-our-jobs kind.

At 50,000 members, Islam is the second largest faith group in the country (compared to four million Christians), and even though they've come here for the same reasons as the Poles and the Nigerians, it's far too tempting to regard them as different to the others. After all, all we hear about Islam is bombings and beheadings and people getting shot for drawing cartoons. People get stoned to death. Women aren't allowed to drive. It seems an intense and forbidding religion. It's frightening.

Of course, a lot of this is based on lack of knowledge. We tend to think of Muslims as one homogenous group rather than people from different countries with different cultures. We don't consider that, like Christianity, Islam has many competing versions.

But this, combined with the regular spewing of horrific images from various parts of the world, is enough to foster at best a mild suspicion, and at worst, fevered conspiracy theories that they are here as part of a plot to outbreed us so they can introduce Sharia law from Ballymun to Ballyhaunis. *Every* time the subject comes up on my radio show, it prompts texts and emails of this sort. Hopefully this is not representative of Ireland as a whole, but these messages come with such regularity that it is worrying.

In 2014, Dr James Carr produced a study entitled *Experiences of Anti-Muslim Racism in Ireland*. It was based on 345 interviews with Muslim men and women from a diverse range of backgrounds, both Irish and foreign. The findings were stark. More than half felt they had experienced hostility, with 22 per cent reporting physical assaults. They were struck, spat at or had hijabs forcibly removed (often with the stated aim of 'liberating' the wearer). Because of the way they dress, Muslim women are more easily identifiable and therefore more vulnerable to these attacks: 40 per cent of females said they had experienced some form of hostility as opposed to 22 per cent of males. This wasn't based on skin colour. Irish converts to Islam (again, mostly women) reported being told that they were 'traitors'.

Here, it seems, we have let ourselves down. While our figures on racism in general are below international norms, when it comes to hostility to Muslims, we're as bad as any other European country.

So we're pretty good at how we treat our minorities except when it comes to Muslims.

And Travellers.

Yes, we were bound to get to this. Not that we like to talk about it much. It's not a popular subject. Like teenagers avoiding homework, Irish society would rather do anything than address the problematic relationship between Travellers and the settled community. Quite rightly, the media and our politicians regularly express concern over racism and how newcomers to our country are treated. There are myriad organisations and academics devoting their time to the welfare of migrants. Yet the Travelling community in Ireland – a group that has existed here for a millennium – gets nothing like this level of care and attention.

Let's start with some facts. There are around 30,000 Travellers in the Republic of Ireland, the vast majority of whom (84 per cent) live in houses. Of the remainder, around half live in caravans and mobile homes that are permanently parked. Most Travellers don't travel. A quarter of them are married by the age of 24. By the age of 15, two-thirds of them have left school. Nearly three-quarters of male Travellers are unemployed and their life expectancy is 61.7 years – more than 15 years behind the general population. The suicide rate among Travellers is six times higher than in the settled population. Compared to the average settled person, the average Traveller is poorer, unhealthier, less educated, more likely to be involved in criminality, more depressed and far less liked.

These facts, admittedly, aren't good, and tend to depict Travellers as a Problem that needs a Solution. It implies that perhaps the issue to be tackled is simply one of poverty. This is not a narrative that Traveller representative groups are particularly keen on. Their position is that the fraught relationship between settled people and Travellers is predicated on racism – a claim that has more than a nugget of truth to it, yet is far from the whole truth.

How can Irish people be racist to Travellers if they are also Irish? Well, because they claim to be an ethnic minority just like any of the other groups we've mentioned.

No one knows when Travellers diverged from mainstream Ireland, other than that it happened a long time ago. Studies of the Traveller language, Gammon or Cant, are inconclusive. Some claim it is an adapted form of Hiberno-English. Others say it contains elements that may predate the Irish language. Some historians claim there is evidence of nomadic groups in Ireland from as early as the fifth century. What's clear is that as long as the Travelling community has existed, it has tended to marry within the group and developed a separate culture informed by their nomadic lifestyle.

Traveller society is patriarchal and favours large families. Because of the traditional ways they earned their living – as travelling tinsmiths, junk dealers or horse renderers – they have inherited a cultural aversion to wage labour. To be a man in Traveller culture means to be self-employed and to provide for your family. As nomads, their view of the world is transitory and somewhat insecure. You're only as rich as the last deal, which is why Travellers spend what money they have on something they can take with them: jewellery, trailers and vans.

They tend to be devout Catholics and have all sorts of rituals peculiar to them, covering everything from washing to death. The balance of academic opinion is that this all adds up to a culture distinctly separate from that of Ireland. Many of the things that settled Irish people value – security, a steady job, a nice home – Travellers abhor.

That's why the 20th century – why modernity – was a catastrophe for Travelling people. There simply wasn't a demand for the kind of business they did any more. There wasn't room for people who didn't want to buy a house and have 2.4 kids, for people who wanted to move from place to

place. From the settled community there was a profound lack
of understanding of this, even a suspicion of anyone who
would want to live that way. Yet the only response the state
could come up with was to build halting sites or, preferably,
make Travellers live in houses like everyone else.

Just like the question about the supposed Celtic origins
of the Irish, DNA can tell us just how different Travellers are
from other people on this island. A genetics expert from the
University of Edinburgh concluded that Travellers diverged
from other Irish people at least 1,000 years ago, making them
a distinct genetic group, as different as Icelanders are from
Norwegians.

This ethnic difference is important in a political sense.
Protection for minorities is enshrined in international law and
various international agreements, and such recognition would
put considerable pressure on the government to do more for
Travellers. But successive governments haven't done it. This is
despite the fact that the UN Committee on the Elimination of
Racial Discrimination and the Council of Europe have called
on the Irish state to do so, and that they were recognised as a
racial group in Northern Ireland in 1997 and in Britain in 2000.

In fairness, various politicians have said the change should
be made, and at the end of 2014, South Dublin County Council
did vote for recognition. But it's also fair to say that there's been
a marked reluctance about it all, because Travellers don't have
much political clout, and because a significant proportion of
the settled community, perhaps even most of them, don't feel
they should be afforded this special status.

If you're Irish, you'll know the reasons why. Travellers don't
work and sponge everything off the state. They beg. Those who

do have an income don't pay any tax. Those who live on halting sites let them become filthy. They dump rubbish everywhere. And then there's the criminality: the theft, the organised gangs, the vicious inter-Traveller feuds with slash-hooks and hurleys, the murders. It can seem as if Travellers don't regard themselves as bound by the rules that the rest of us are.

Now of course these are crass generalisations, bordering on defamation. But it is how Travellers are widely *perceived* by the rest of society, and this is not *just* down to racial stereotyping. There is a problem of criminality within the Travelling community, and it's disingenuous to pretend otherwise.

But crime and anti-social behaviour aren't simply caused by people being bad. The evidence from every nation on earth is that there is *always* a connection between crime and poverty, and to all the powerlessness that comes from being poor. What's astounding is how little has been done to study this. When researching this book, I was awash with various reports about how migrants fare in Ireland. When it comes to Travellers, there are far fewer, and those studies that have been produced don't get nearly as much play in the media. Ireland thinks about Travellers when there's a news report about a row at a wedding. The rest of the time there's a relentless silence.

Two studies have been produced in relation to Travellers in prison. One was conducted in Ireland in 2014 and found that a disproportionate number of Travellers are incarcerated. Men are between five and 11 times more likely to be jailed, while for women it's 18 to 22 times more likely. A 2005 study looking at mental health among Travellers claimed that they make up 5.4 per cent of the Irish prison population, while only comprising 0.6 per cent of the population as a whole.

A study carried out in the UK in 2011 reckoned that Travellers make up 1 per cent of the prison population in England and Wales – a massive disparity given that the general population is 56 million and that there are only 15,000 Travellers (that's 0.026785714285714288 per cent of the population). Both studies found evidence of racism towards them in prison, along with problems related to literacy (they can't get help because they can't fill out forms). The British study claimed that over 50 per cent of Travellers in prison can't read adequately and that one-quarter suffered from mental health problems. And just in case you're wondering, most were in for crimes of theft.

Look at it this way: Travellers are a lost people. We live in the age of the internet, yet they still cling to a culture where a man provides for his family by selling scrap metal. Some anthropological studies of Traveller language have found it telling, and perhaps poignant, that their language seems to have ceased inventing any new words. Culturally, they are stuck in a past where 16-year-old boys are expected to act like men, to eschew education and to make their way by trading and living on their wits. But the world doesn't work like that any more, and it hasn't for some time. But rather than viewing their predicament with empathy, rather than trying to help them make the adjustment to the way things are now, we act like they disgust us.

The veteran sociologist Dr Micheál Mac Gréil has for many years tracked the tides of intolerance in Ireland, and he reports that from the 1970s it has increased markedly towards Travellers. In 2011, the statistics were that 60 per cent of people would not welcome a Traveller into their family, 40 per cent would not employ a Traveller and almost 20 per cent *would deny them citizenship.* We don't want to work alongside them, or have our kids marry them, or see them in our bars or restaurants, or have them live anywhere near us. We don't want to see them or think about them. It's Irish-style apartheid, and we're the white people.

There have been many occasions when we've almost had a public discussion about this, but somehow we've always managed to avoid it. When the farmer Padraig Nally shot dead the Traveller John Ward, who had been attempting rob Nally's house, the majority of the media scrambled away from it, understandably fearful of establishing a Settled versus Traveller debate. Instead, we had no debate at all.

Well, not about Travellers anyway. The tragedy of the Nally/ Ward case (and it was tragic for both men and their families) did prompt discussion about the difficulties and dangers for people living in remote parts of Ireland, about the closures of Garda stations and post offices and how the drink-driving laws are apparently denuding rural communities. This brings us to another element in our exploration of Irish agreeableness: the trust part.

We've already dealt with how Irish people are wary of intimacy. We drink so we can share our feelings and not have them reported back to us the next day. We don't like to talk about money. We have a tendency to assume (and often with good reason) that people who do well have done so because of who they know rather than pure merit. But that's wariness. When it comes to our national institutions, however, it flowers into full-blown suspicion.

The Edelman Trust Barometer annually tracks public trust in 27 countries. According to the 2015 results, we are the second least trusting country, just in front of Japan. We show precious little trust in government or the media or banks, and what trust there is has been declining over the past few years.

But given what's happened in this country since 2008, that's no great surprise. Government, the media, the church, business – all of them have spectacularly failed our society and to a greater or lesser extent have operated only out of their own self-interest. *Plus ça change*, you might say if you were given to using fancy French phrases. Ordinary people have always (and rightly so) been suspicious of the rich and powerful. Seán Ó Faoláin wrote in his 1947 book *The Irish* that native Irish chieftains often found it difficult to command the loyalty of their subjects, who regarded them as not much better than the Normans or any other invaders. But Ó Faoláin argued that distrust came from more than just poor governance. It was a survival strategy, borne out of dealing with war, poverty and invasion – of never quite knowing who your allies were: 'We expect guile from one another as we expect rain from the skies.' It's a function of something we've touched on before: that we are a small country and have to be careful about how much we reveal to each other.

Ó Faoláin also argued that for many centuries we had an undeveloped sense of nationhood. We were aware of the Irish being one people, but (once again) in a contradictory way: 'they seem to have had no difficulty in combining this strong sense of their racial oneness with an equally strong insistence on their regional otherness; which ultimately seems to have nourished the fatal delusion that to flourish as a people it was not necessary to formulate the political concept of the nation'. Nationalism as a concept didn't arrive until many centuries later.

The point here is that local ties in Ireland have far deeper historical roots than national ones. Ó Faoláin claimed that even up to the 17th century, the Irish had a 'claustrophobic horror' of towns and tended to burn them down whenever the opportunity arose, which brings us back to what *was* discussed after the Ward/Nally case: the urban–rural split in Ireland.

It's always been there. For centuries, rural Ireland has maintained a profound suspicion of Dublin – traditionally the power base of whoever was ruling Ireland at the time (Ó Faoláin also makes the point that most towns in Ireland were originally established by invaders). For its part, Dublin has viewed the rest of the country with, at best, bemusement.

What's new, though, is how the numbers have flipped. Ireland was a rural country with a city bolted onto the side of it. Thanks to the Celtic Tiger, most people now live in urban areas, or at least some of the statistics claim this. According to the Irish definition of 'urban', more than 60 per cent of us live in towns and cities. But some international studies say it's below 30 per cent. A study published in 2013 claimed that Ireland has the most rural economy in Europe, and that our urban–rural split is the most extreme.

It's this last point that is the most important here. Regardless of how we define 'urban', the money still flows to the east coast. Most multinationals locate within an hour's drive of the capital. Dublin contains 27 per cent of the population, but it accounts for 40 per cent of the economic output and 40 per cent of the jobs. The perception outside the city is that Dublin gets everything – that most of the economic and political power is centred there and that it works for the benefit of Dublin. We'll go into this in more detail in a subsequent chapter, but this has had a toxic effect on our political system. Ó Faoláin said that we were slow to develop a concept of the nation. It is arguable that we still haven't got there. *Irish Times* columnist Fintan O'Toole has written that Ireland 'is a state to which many of its decent respectable inhabitants feel no attachment whatsoever'. This certainly seems to be the case in terms of how the Irish regard their capital city. A survey conducted by Dublin City Council in 2010 found that only 26 per cent of people feel any emotional attachment to the city, and that figures drops to 15 per cent when you exclude Dubliners.

Dublin contains more green spaces than any other European city. It's got the Dáil, the GPO, Áras an Uachtaráin, universities, Croke Park, the Aviva Stadium and four Nobel prizes for literature. And 74 per cent of the country couldn't give a damn about it. It is the capital, but not *their* capital. Ireland was once a patchwork of kingdoms, and to a certain extent it still is. In the late 1980s, studies were conducted that asked people to self-identify. About one-third put down their county or province *first* and Irish second.

This is an odd memory, but I'll give it to you anyway. I must have been around 14, and for reasons I can't remember now, I was in Dublin with my parents. My father and I went to use the toilet, and already standing at the urinal was a man in a CIÉ (now Dublin Bus) uniform. There was some sort of industrial dispute going on at the time, and because my dad was one of those people who would talk to you while were standing at a urinal, he asked the man about it.

The man gave a long and, to my father at least, interesting answer, so much so that after he had left my father declared, as if this was something he had forgotten but was happy to be reminded of: 'Dubliners are very friendly.'

I can remember being distinctly shocked by this. Even though I had been living in Ballinasloe for only a couple of years, I had already been deeply imprinted with the prevailing idea that Dublin was a pitiless, miserable town, filled for the most part with thugs who spoke an incomprehensible patois, and who, when not signing on for the dole, would vary their schedule of drinking themselves insensible by occasionally robbing a shop or kicking each other.

But that was the 1970s, when, admittedly, Dublin was a bit more run down. Now the narrative is that it's full of snooty Dublin 4 types who look down their noses at the culchies.

I'm being a bit glib, but the division is real, and is informed in part by what social anthropologists refer to as a post-colonial inferiority complex – the insidious idea that even though independence from the empire has been won, we might have been better off staying where we were, that we are not quite *as good* as our former colonial masters. It's like a political Stockholm syndrome. We fight to be free, but when we achieve that freedom we miss our old captors and can't quite rid ourselves of the idea that their approval is what's most important.

This theory has been discussed in most post-colonial countries in the world, including Ireland. But some have argued that it is particularly acute here because we have the misfortune to be located right beside the old coloniser. We've been able to look across the Irish Sea at the Brits and witness how badly we're doing by comparison.

How this relates to the urban–rural split can be summed up in the term *West Brit* – the centuries-old suspicion that the further east you went, the less *Irish* the people were and the more they looked towards London to get their cultural guidance.

The gravitational pull of London is all but gone, but on the east coast it has been replaced by the sort of internationalism that we talked about in the previous chapter.

In 2004, I interviewed a man on Newstalk who was the organiser of the Athlone Agricultural Show because they were having a competition to find Ireland's largest root vegetable. All a bit of harmless fun. But what was shocking afterwards (and Newstalk was a Dublin-only station at the time) was the enormous number of text and email messages criticising the man's accent. *He's like a Father Ted character. It's embarrassing. Why would you put someone like that on the air?*

In fairness, it was a minority, but there was still a sizable cohort that felt that this kind of *Irishness* should be done away with, like a shameful family secret we should never talk about.

Back in those days another regular contributor to the show was the academic Terry Dolan, the author of *A Dictionary of Hiberno-English.* Terry regularly explained that the so-called DART accent in Dublin is in fact far older than the rail service it exists along. His analysis was that it was an attempt by well-to-do Dubliners to ape English Received Pronunciation. So, here is the post-colonial inferiority complex in action. Feeling inferior, middle-class Dubliners attempt to speak more like English people – a change in accent that is an implicit (and sometimes explicit) judgement on the people outside the Pale who speak differently. In turn, those people feel inferior and resentful. As a result, they feel that Dublin isn't really their city or their capital; it's barely in their country.

Nowadays, none of this is a conscious process. It's an historical hangover. In the 21st century, the barrage of various media is also having an effect in flattening out the Irish accent, particularly among younger people. Yet it's still striking how few regional accents you hear in the broadcast media. If you live outside Dublin, you don't hear anyone like you. So of course it's the *Dublin* media. And sometimes it displays how Dublin-centric it is. When, in 2009, the government proposed new drink-driving limits for the completely legitimate purpose of saving lives, there was a threatened backbench revolt from many rural TDs. This was at a time when the country was facing into the first of a series of brutal budgets, so the Dublin media was full of snippy comments on how these TDs (some of whom were publicans) seemed more concerned about defending the rights of their constituents to have a few pints and drive home rather than cuts to carers' allowances or resource teachers in schools. It was portrayed as a typical example of *Irish* doublethink. Yet what the media didn't get was the central role of the pub in Irish rural life – that it is a part of our culture and has been for a very long time. It wasn't about drink. It was about defending communities, about giving people a place to go and meet each other. The new regulations were passed and undoubtedly saved lives, but thousands of rural pubs have also closed. Outside Dublin, isolation is a very real problem.

I could go on. There's a long list of examples of how Dublin and the rest of the country seem to fail to understand each other. But I'll limit myself to just two more.

The first is the story of the Quinn family. But to understand the conflicting views about them, you've also got to understand the enormous effect that the Quinn Group had on Cavan and the border counties.

Despite the massive wealth he accrued – he was at one time the richest man in Ireland – Sean Quinn was a rural Irish success story. He grew up on a 23-acre farm in County Fermanagh and, like his brother Peter, was embedded in that most Irish of organisations, the GAA.

More than any other Irish institution, the GAA has managed the trick of being expansively national and minutely local at the same time. It is at the heart of numerous communities around the country. Indeed, it's easily arguable that were it not for the GAA, those communities might not exist. We might not even have the *counties* as they exist today were it not for the GAA. It was the GAA that created inter-county rivalry through hurling and football teams and thus fostered a sense of self-identity in areas that previously had been little more than administrative units based on arbitrary barony boundaries.

This strong sense of local identity has always been in Ireland in various forms. But it was the GAA that gave it the shape it has today. It's had a profound effect on the country in all sorts of ways, particularly in politics. But we'll come back to that.

So both the Quinns were embedded in the GAA, and as a result embedded in their community. And they stayed. Sean launched a gravel business from the farm with a loan of £100 and from there diversified into cement, hotels, glass, insurance and all sorts of investments overseas. At the height of the Quinn Group, Sean was worth around €4.7 billion, employing over 5,000 people. Yet still he stayed. The house was big and fancy, of course, but it was in Cavan, just a few miles down the road from where he grew up. He was providing jobs there.

This was a part of Ireland, like most of the border counties, that felt a million miles away from the capital, economically and politically. Dublin had done nothing for Cavan. But Sean Quinn had. And he was one of their own.

Not only did he provide jobs and money, but he gave a sense of confidence to the area – a hope that it could succeed. And it could do so locally, without any handouts from Dublin.

Then it all went horribly wrong when his dodgy punt on Anglo-Irish Bank curdled. The courts went after him and the Quinns twisted on the hook. To the Dublin media, and much of the country, this was an already familiar story of the greedy rich ruining the country. Pictures of Gucci-clad family members and stories about high-priced cakes and payments to and from companies all over Europe only added to the juicy depiction of the Quinns as archetypal Celtic Puppies: rich, smug, morally lax and deserving of their place on the baddies' list along with bankers, property developers and most politicians – the people we had come to blame for the state of the country.

But for supporters of the Quinn family back home, Sean was a victim. He had simply made a bad investment, but was now being vilified for it. The same baddies – bankers, property developers, most politicians – this time aided by the media, were simply trying to divert the blame away from themselves and onto the Quinns. And why wouldn't they think that? They *knew* this man, and all they knew of Dublin was that it had ignored them since the foundation of the state.

It didn't really matter that Quinn's attempt to portray himself as a victim was, to put it mildly, disingenuous. The point was that this was an attack not just on him, but on the community he came from. No doubt the Quinns still feel bitter about their experience. So, too, do many people in the border counties.

But let's leave bitterness behind in favour of loveliness. Every year, Ireland seems to have the same conversation about the Rose of Tralee competition. It's broadcast over two nights, it goes on for hours, and in 2014, half of all people watching television in Ireland watched the Rose. Culturally, and in terms of the television business, that's a phenomenal statistic. Yet every August there's a PR skirmish between supporters of the competition and those who would rather it didn't exist. In recent years the competition seems to have been getting the edge, with the organisers arguing that it's about rural Ireland and connecting with the Irish diaspora, that critics of such a noble project don't understand rural Ireland – that they are metropolitan cultural snobs. And no one wants to be accused of that.

Criticism of the Rose seems to have two main planks. Firstly, it's twee and unendurably naff, an impression ingrained in the public mind not just by the competition itself but also by how it was sent up by the TV show *Father Ted* as the Lovely Girls Competition.

The second criticism is that it is, essentially, a beauty contest. Granted, there is no swimsuit section and there is a focus on what the women do for a living and what talents they may have, yet it is still a parade of young single women vying for approval.

The first objection is simply a matter of taste. Most cultures have naff aspects to them (try watching German or Italian TV). If you don't like it, don't look at it.

It's the second criticism that's more difficult to dismiss. It *is* a series of women seeking approval. It's disingenuous to pretend that how they look is irrelevant to how they do in the competition. The organisers say it's a celebration of Irish womanhood. Yet getting these women to compete against one another – no matter how convivial the atmosphere – is an odd form of celebration.

Nevertheless, two halves of the country seem to view the Rose of Tralee in wildly differing ways. No, I'm not a fan. I do find it twee and, as television entertainment, a bit boring. But I've sat with people who have enjoyed it, and they have done so in exactly the way the organisers describe. (The Rose is perfect for the way many Irish people consume television. They have conversations while it's on in the background so they can occasionally refer to what's on the screen.) For those people, it wasn't about relative degrees of beauty or what dresses the contestants wore, but what their *story* was: where they were from, who their family was – the key referents of rural life. In rural Ireland, *place* is crucially important, as it can tell you all about a person's background and, more importantly, start the process of forming a link between you and them. People at home hear a surname and a townland and start asking themselves if they know anyone with that name in that county.

For the Roses from abroad, there is the added zing of the emigrant's tale: of the family forced to leave, yet who kept the culture alive, who produced an American- or Australian-sounding daughter who can play the fiddle or do a jig. Viewers in Ireland watch contestants from other countries who are, arguably, more 'Irish' than the viewers are.

It brings the emigrant's story to a Hollywood-esque conclusion: returned at last, and this time fêted by the old country. All the historical wrongs finally put right. It is the nostalgia-drenched dream of an immutable, innocent Ireland – the version de Valera wanted but without all the poverty and priests and narrow-mindedness. As a television show, this isn't the grammar of a beauty contest, but of reality TV. Just like in *The X Factor*, it's much more emotionally satisfying for the audience to root for a winner who has had some hardship to overcome. It is perhaps telling that in the history of the competition, 33 of the winners have come from abroad while 23 have come from Ireland. Only five have come from Dublin. It is cheesy, irony free and jarringly wholesome, but it uses such powerful tropes (the returned emigrant, the *cóilean deas*) that it appeals to the racial and personal memories of hundreds of thousands of people. In TV terms, it's quite brilliant, and uniquely Irish. Or rural Irish.

But then, in 2014, something remarkable happened. That year's winner, Maria Walsh, revealed that she was gay, and suddenly the Rose of Tralee could make a legitimate claim to modernity, especially as the country wasn't too far away from taking a vote on legalising same-sex marriage. Most interesting of all was the reaction to her announcement. There was a rash of positive news reports and that was about it. No backlash, no tut-tutting even from the most conservative elements. The Rose of Tralee was a lesbian and it *wasn't a big deal*. A symbol of the 'old' Ireland had managed to morph into a symbol of the 'new' Ireland. The rural had shown itself, at least in this respect, to be every bit as progressive as the urban. And the urban had to grudgingly accept that this was a good thing.

So, we're divided, we're suspicious. We are, towards certain groups, profoundly racist. But of course we are contradictory – and this aspect of our nature is both exasperating and redeeming.

In 2014 a former British policy advisor named Simon Anholt decided to devise a different way of judging how countries perform, not just economically or militarily or how they wield hard or soft power. He used 35 separate indicators from the World Bank and the UN in areas such as equality, health, science, culture and the environment. He called it – with tongue ever-so-slightly poking in his cheek – the Good Country Index, with the aim of trying to rate what each country contributes to the common good of humanity and what it takes away. It was a close-run thing (Finland put up a hell of a fight), but when he totted up all the points, Anholt found that Ireland came out top. We are the 'goodest' country in the world.

It's quite reasonable to view such polls sceptically, but in the simple endeavour of helping people in other countries, Ireland does do extraordinarily well. This statement comes heavily qualified, but most of the time the Irish are kind.

Ireland is respected for its overseas aid work, and while you'd have to be smoking something hugely potent to fancy Ireland as a military power, our army does have a sterling reputation abroad for myriad involvements in UN operations.

In the 1980s, I was in southern Lebanon and saw how the Irish battalion based in Tibnin had managed to bring peace and comfort to an area that had been smashed to pieces by Israeli invasions and a devastating civil war. Their main job at the time was to marshal the South Lebanon Army (SLA)

– a group funded and armed by Israel (to oppose the PLO) whose members were notoriously undisciplined and prone to torturing people. The SLA would set up roadblocks, and in response the Irish would set up roadblocks on either side of them. This was not something that particularly pleased the SLA, but under the UN terms of engagement, the Irish couldn't close them down or fire at them unless they were fired upon first. Essentially, they let themselves be targets, and sometimes the SLA (and the Israelis) couldn't resist the temptation.

Yet the mission wasn't about guns, at least in the way the Irish Army went about it. Their main weapon was charm. Irish soldiers would routinely diffuse tensions by wandering over to the SLA men to have a chat, and for the most part this worked.

Despite the risks, the Irish soldiers did all this in an astoundingly good-natured manner. I was in my early twenties at the time, and I met men even younger than me carrying out this work. I met older, more grizzled veterans who had been on all sorts of operations in the region – guarding buildings and evacuating areas and holding bleeding civilians together while they waited for the medics to arrive. One man told me how he was given the task of surveying an area after a particularly bloody battle. They had to figure out which body parts belonged to which side.

I am, by nature, suspicious of patriotism. Irish history has somewhat poisoned the word, and all too often it can lead to mawkish, chauvinistic jingoism. But during that trip I was aware of a swelling sense of pleasure in my nationality – of men and women working at something because it was a *good* thing to do.

It gets even better. There is an aspect of life in which the Irish are, in my opinion, the kindest, the most pro-social and the most agreeable: death.

The rituals we have built up around funerals, or at least some of them, date from pre-Christian times, when mourners would remain with the body until it was buried. Whether by chance or historical evolution, it is tempting to believe that there is an ancient wisdom to it. Like doctors or the fire brigade, you can't quite appreciate it until you've been in the centre of this process yourself.

My father died suddenly in 2011. I knew it would happen sooner or later; everyone with an elderly parent considers the possibility. Yet when it arrived, the thudding shock of it seemed to dislocate everything. I was an adult, but he was still my dad and I was still a son. He was part of my mental map of the world, containing all the places I live and visit and all the people I now realise I consider permanent fixtures. He is still in that map, of course, and curiously, my images of him are now more vivid than ever. But they have changed too – darkened.

Helen and I docilely stepped through the preparations, a script already written for us and already performed by millions of others: the burial plot, the casket, the mass readings. We stood in a room as people filed past. They glanced into a coffin that contained what seemed to be a facsimile of my father – a grim waxwork parody. They shook our hands and made their whispered comments: *I'm sorry for your trouble. I'm sorry for your loss. I was only talking to him the other day.*

As the cliché goes, there is nothing you can say to someone in grief, certainly not anything to take away the pain. But these old phrases have the dignified function of reminding the griever that they are not alone – that these friends and neighbours would, if they could, willingly help shoulder the distress. And this does help. At funerals, you see Irish people at their very best.

Another cliché: emotional roller-coaster. At funerals, tragedy abuts comedy. My father died at home, so the horrendous task of lifting him into a temporary coffin was followed by a brief panic over locating his false teeth. At the removal, the harrowed tears of his grandchildren were preceded by two hours during which an unsettling number of people said to me, *It was so sudden. And you look just like him.*

The day of the funeral, I woke up early. Grief robs you of sleep when you most need it, in my case by delivering repeated dreams of my father in which he would be sitting the way he always did or using one of his favourite phrases. And then I would remember that he was gone.

I went for a walk around the town, eventually arriving at the church where my father lay, where people were streaming in for early mass – there, so many of them told me, to pray for Frank; Irish people at their very best.

When it was all over, depleted of energy by the day's events, we sat in a hotel and eventually began to say our goodnights. My father's brother, then 81 and now also dead, was heading back to his room when he collapsed. He became confused and fiercely resisted all our attempts to coax him into the ambulance we had called. I kneeled in front of him and reassured him that I would go with him to the hospital – that I would not leave his side. But it wasn't my words that calmed him down, it was what so many people had said to me at the removal. Still addled, he looked back at me and said, *Yes, Frank.*

Chapter 4

The Lives of Others: How Conscientious Are We?

I can't remember how many times I've been on the dole. But I remember the last occasion, in 1996. That summer I'd presented a chat show on RTÉ called *Good Grief Moncrieff*. Because I was a relative newcomer it had generated a lot of advance publicity. This was seen as a bold step for the broadcaster as I was to be temporarily replacing *Kenny Live*.

The amount of hype it received in advance was equalled by the amount of excoriation it got during the run. It was a failure. To this day I still don't know who took the decision to give me the gig. Certainly the RTÉ executive who told me about it said that in his opinion I wasn't ready yet for a show like this, but given that the offer had come from 'upstairs', I had no option but to accept. And he was right. I had to accept – and I wasn't ready. The show was loud and ragged and I was nervous for most of the run. During show two – during which

I'd interviewed a woman who talked a bit too vividly about her sex change operation – the switchboard logged a record number of complaints. The following week a producer told me that RTÉ was looking for an increase in the license fee and that I was responsible for making that task more difficult.

When the series came to an end, a few people said that I was bound to be offered another show given that they had invested so much in me, and I was keen to believe them. But nothing came, and within a few months I found myself down in the dole office, explaining my situation to a puzzled-looking man. He didn't say it explicitly, though it was clear he couldn't quite come to grips with my presence there. *Why do you need the dole? You're off the telly.*

Thankfully, it didn't last long. I got another gig in RTÉ. But I kept the social welfare card in my wallet for many years afterwards, just to remind myself.

Before that, I was on the dole at least a couple of times in the early 1980s, and those experiences were completely different. It was rather jolly, because pretty much everyone I knew was or had been claiming. I was a freelance journalist and the income from that was patchy at best. The dole was a resource and I didn't give one second's thought to where that money came from or if I was really entitled to it. I didn't pay tax on anything I made from journalism either, and insofar as I thought about it (which wasn't very much), I had a dull sense that I was taking the money from some grey, authoritarian body that didn't really care about me – that claiming the dole and not paying tax was even a sort of revolutionary act. I can remember, after a trip abroad, wondering how I would explain to the dole office that I had a tan. But they never asked.

I was young and unthinking, but my general attitude towards the state was not unusual, then and now. I didn't feel a need to be conscientious towards it because I didn't really feel it had anything to do with me, or others like me. Those in authority, those who handed out the dole, were Other. This sense of Otherness is deeply ingrained in Irish culture. The British, Dublin, politicians, various arms of the state – they are all Other and therefore don't deserve respect or trust. For a small country, we are curiously infected with the idea that we are *not* all in it together, and this has profoundly affected how, collectively and individually, we think about Ireland. It affects how we act too. Why should I be conscientious if you are not?

But of course – in the typically contradictory Irish way – people on the dole are also Other. This sense became even more acute during the boom, when the unemployed were suspected (by some) of simply being lazy, and during the crash, when the enormous drain on the social welfare budgets was seen (by some) as part of the economic problem. One interesting aspect of the crash is how it seemed to override traditional Irish guilt. We didn't blame ourselves for what happened – we blamed each other.

Dole fraud, or the perception of it, has become politically fraught in Ireland since the crash, and this seems to be because of a change of attitude towards it in Irish society. It's not so jolly any more. In 2008, there were 1,044 anonymous tip-offs of alleged social welfare fraud phoned in to the department, but by 2011 that number had swelled to 16,917 and to 28,022 in 2012. Since then the numbers have dropped back a bit, to 21,088 in 2014.

However, this doesn't mean that dole fraud increased dramatically over the last few years, just that there was an increased *perception* of it going on. There's no detail on how many of the tip-offs led to prosecutions or changes in social welfare payments. Of the 21,088 tip-offs in 2014, about two-thirds were referred for 'further investigation'.

Nonetheless, the fact that so many people felt the need to phone in their suspicions does signal a significant change: a final realisation that tax money is 'our' money to be used for the collective good of society. This is a huge shift, given the traditional Irish horror of informing.

That's the positive interpretation. The negative one is that it's evidence of a new meanness in Ireland, a willingness to blame anyone else for the economic debacle – in this case, to blame the poor. This has been fuelled, at least in part, by regular, breathless *Daily Mail*-style headlines about individual cases of dole fraud or the huge numbers phoning the hotline. The Department of Social Protection doesn't say how many of these tip-offs are legitimate, but it does produce a Fraud and Error Report, and according to figures from May 2014, about 2 per cent of social welfare claims are fraudulent – in line with pretty much every other country in Europe. Based on the February 2015 unemployment figures, that's around 7,000 people.

The truth is perhaps a mixture of these two interpretations. There is an increase of conscientiousness towards public monies *and* an increase in meanness. But when I say meanness, you may say *realism* or even *political ideology*. We'll come back to this, but Ireland does seem to have shifted to the right politically over the last few years. Or maybe it was always this way. In *The Irish* (and remember, he was writing in the 1940s), Seán Ó Faoláin claimed that the party that became Fine Gael 'were the sponsors of the form of society that was to set the broad pattern of Irish life ever since: one based on a philosophy of *laissez faire* qualified only, and happily, by the creation of such publicly owned enterprises as communications, radio, electricity, sugar and transport by air, rail and road'. You can count up yourself how many of those have now fallen into private hands. There is an old saying in Irish politics that people think left, but vote right.

'Left' and 'right' mean different things in different parts of the world. In this context it means *centre*-left and *centre*-right, like most European countries. The main differences are how much capitalism is subject to regulation and how much of a social safety net is provided by the state. Crudely put, the further north you go in Europe, the better the safety net is and the more equal those societies are. This is important because more equal societies do better.

In 2009, the British epidemiologists Richard Wilkinson and Kate Pickett published their book *The Spirit Level: Why More Equal Societies Almost Always do Better*. Based on years of international research, it argued that in the areas of physical health, mental health, drug abuse, education, imprisonment, obesity, social mobility, trust and community life, violence, teenage pregnancies and child well-being, outcomes are significantly worse in more unequal rich countries. The more unequal a society is, the more it is anxious, unhealthy and untrusting. In 2013, the French economist Thomas Piketty made similar claims in his book *Capital in the Twenty-First Century* – adding that this growing inequality threatens democracy.

Income inequality is generally calculated using a measure called the Gini co-efficient, which was developed in the early 20th century by the Italian statistician and sociologist Corrado Gini. Later in life, Gini was a fascist, a eugenicist and the founder of a political party that wanted a world government led by the US. But his maths seem to have been unaffected by his loony political ideas. Basically, it measures how much money a society earns and the relative shares of that income pie.

It can be calculated in slightly different ways, but income inequality has been steadily on the rise in Ireland since 1980. From the 1990s, the income of the top 1 per cent has risen sharply, meaning they were taking a much larger slice than everyone else. From 1975 to the height of the boom in 2006, average gross incomes more than doubled, for the top 10 per cent it tripled and for the top 1 per cent it went up by a factor of five. According to figures produced by the Think-Tank for Action on Social Change (TASC) in 2015, the top 10 per cent earn 33 per cent of the income. The rich got richer, and the recession doesn't seem to have affected that. In fact, things have got better for them. *The Sunday Times Rich List* in 2015 calculated that Ireland's wealthy are now better off than they were at the height of the Celtic Tiger. According to the paper, the 250 richest individuals have a combined worth of €75 billion, equivalent to 30 per cent of Ireland's GDP.

What it does show, however, is that the economic rising tide did raise all (or most) boats, just not at an equal rate. While we are one of the most unequal countries in Europe based on gross pay, when taxation and social welfare payments are included – when some of the wealth is redistributed – we fall back to close to the European average. So we're not that bad. We're not great, though. TASC warns that the longer the gap is left, the harder it is to make up. Redistributing the wealth might sound nice to lefty types, but it runs the risk of building up social welfare dependency. It's arguable that we've done that already.

There is an underclass in Ireland, and it's always been there. But it tends to be one of those issues that doesn't get much attention in our public discussions. Rather like politics in the US, Irish politics gives most of its attention to the middle classes, because that's where most of the votes are. You get a big chunk of the middle classes behind you, and you can ignore the poor. Not only that – you can attach a moral weight to their poverty. During the boom in particular, there was the widespread and insidious idea that unemployment had become a choice – that some were too lazy and too well cosseted by the state to bother working. In 1999, a Freedom of Information request by the *Sunday Times* revealed a letter from an assistant secretary at the Department of Justice in which he claimed that the poverty figures for Ireland were exaggerated by the 'poverty industry'.

Such ideas are not unique to Ireland, of course. But what is peculiar to us is the persistent myth that we have a 'classless' society. If Ireland is classless, then everyone, no matter what their socio-economic status when they start out, has a pretty good chance of getting on in life.

It's utter nonsense. It's always been nonsense. It's an idea that's been promulgated for the past 100 years or so by people keen to make distinctions between the Irish and the British. Certainly we don't have an aristocracy, but we've always had the poor and the middle classes. In his 2011 book *Privileged Lives: A Social History of Middle-Class Ireland 1882–1989*, the historian Tony Farmar goes into forensic detail as to what the Irish middle classes ate, where they lived, how they spent their money and what kind of jobs they did. Every urban area in Ireland is defined by a series of invisible borders that divides the working class and the various shades of middle class – and *everyone* in that town or city is aware of them. To be born in a 'rough' area carries with it automatic disadvantage. It will tend to be less aspirational, not to value education as much, to have a higher proportion of unemployed people, to have more crime. Now of course there will always be people who have come from such areas and done well, but the struggle to do so will be more difficult. A study carried out by the *Irish Times* in 2010 found that in secondary schools in Cabra, Ballymun, Finglas and Blanchardstown, between 11 and 14 per cent of students went on to third-level education. The figure for most schools on the south side of Dublin was close to 100 per cent. Similarly, the high-points courses in universities – law and medicine, for instance – have an inordinately high intake of kids from fee-paying schools, yet only around 10 per cent of Irish children attend such schools.

So if you're born into a middle-class home, you're far more likely to end up doing a middle-class job. It may also have an influence on what sport you play. Rugby is uniformly middle class in Ireland, while boxing and soccer are working class. Only the GAA is relatively classless, probably because, in rural areas at least, the player pool is much smaller and discriminating on the grounds of social class would be self-defeating.

One can quibble about what exactly constitutes middle class – and you'd be right to because it is furiously tricky to define. Income doesn't help: it's not uncommon for an electrician to make far more money than a national school teacher. The trades union movement is increasingly made up of middle-class people. Various studies over the last couple of decades have asked people to define what class they belong to. The numbers ranged between 40 to 65 per cent, though in all the surveys, a significant number claimed to be classless.

Education may provide a clue. According to figures released by Eurostat in 2013, Ireland has the highest level of third-level degree attainment in the European Union at 51.1 per cent for 30- to 34-year-olds. (The EU average is 35.8 per cent.) That breaks down to 44 per cent of men and 57.9 per cent among women, which would imply that there are more middle-class women than men.

Most political parties in Ireland seem to work on the assumption that the middle class is the overwhelming majority: an idea that is resisted by left-wing politicians who would prefer to promote the more traditional idea of a large working class. But even they don't use those terms much. The likes of Joe Higgins from the Socialist Party will as often say *working people*: a term that includes most of the adult population. And he may well have a point. 'Middle class' is not that useful as a term, as it takes in the huge swathe of people in between the underclass and the wealthy. Being middle class in Killiney is probably quite different to being middle class in Killarney.

Yet we can't deny that most people in Ireland vote for centre-right parties – the parties that assume the middle class is in the majority. But that's *not* to say that they are all smug and comfortable. Since the financial crash, economists such as David McWilliams have argued that the Irish middle classes have been facing an economic existential threat. Many of them

are just a pay cheque or two away from disaster. Many of them
have found themselves in that disaster.

This middle-class struggle is reflected in society in many
ways, but one is in the way we shop. Currently, around 70
per cent of all grocery shopping in Ireland takes place in
SuperValu, Tesco and Dunnes, and various studies have shown
that for 90 per cent of us, price is the primary concern, which
is also why around two-thirds of shoppers visit more than one
supermarket on a weekly basis and tend to favour 'own-brand'
products. But despite the fact that we are one of the most wired
up – or wireless – nations on earth (the Irish have an average of
3.1 connected devices), we are leery about shopping online. We
do it far less than most other European nations, and four times
less than the British. Indeed, Irish consumers are notably fond
of a practice called 'reverse showrooming'. We will research a
product online and have a good look at it, but we'll go into a
shop to buy it.

It wasn't always like this. The recession prompted a major
change in Irish consumer behaviour. The crash made most of us
far more cautious, and that habit seems to have stuck, even into
2015 when there were signs that the economy was improving.

Which is perhaps another reason why the poor don't get
discussed much. The middle classes have their own problems
to contend with.

Middle class may be difficult to define neatly, but poor is not.
The commonly used term is 'consistent poverty', which is defined
by 11 'deprivation indicators', such as being unable to afford to a
warm waterproof coat or having to turn off the heating due to
lack of money. In 2013, 8.2 per cent of Irish people were poor.
Among the unemployed, the figure was 23.9 per cent. A 2013

study by UNICEF looked at child poverty across 41 developed countries. Ireland was among the worst in 37th place.

Let's remind you of those income disparity figures: the top 10 per cent earn 33 per cent of the income. The bottom 10 per cent get *3 per cent* of the income.

More otherness: to the poor, middle-class Ireland (and uber-rich Ireland; we'll get to them later) is Other. Middle-class values – go to college, get a nice job, play by the rules – don't apply for many poor people because they are unattainable. If you are born into poverty and the likelihood is that you will experience nothing but poverty in the future, such values are nonsensical.

The American sociologist Richard Sennett has written that lack of respect is one of the most significant 'hidden injuries of class', and during the Celtic Tiger, when Ireland spent most of the time patting its own back, the lack of respect towards the poor was palpable. We'd all done fantastically well, and given that Ireland was an opportunity-rich 'classless' society, then why hadn't the poor got off their lazy arses and done the same?

They hadn't because they couldn't – because such opportunities were effectively closed to them. It's perhaps no coincidence that modern organised crime in Ireland became more widespread during the same period that the economy started to improve. For young men, crime and being feared were ways of achieving status when no others were available. In her book *Understanding Limerick: Social Exclusion and Change*, the sociologist Niamh Hourigan wrote that 'this status is linked to being a "hard man" who embodies toughness and a capacity for violence, as a figure who then elicits fear in his more vulnerable neighbours'.

There are a handful of such men who make enormous amounts of money from organised crime. The last Garda count was that there are 25 such gangs in Ireland. But for the most part, the foot soldiers do it for status. A study carried out by the University of Chicago in the 1990s looked at the 'business model' for a crack-dealing gang and found that it was pretty similar to a McDonald's – it was a system of franchises. But the vast majority of 'employees' – the street-level dealers – were earning $3.30 an hour – *less* than they would have at a McDonald's. Within the poor housing projects where these men lived, to be a drug dealer was regarded as 'glamorous' and regarded with respect. Or fear. Either would do.

The discussion of what to do about such criminality pops up every now and again, usually after some gangland shootings or when the latest series of the RTÉ TV crime series *Love/Hate* hits the screens. The proposed solutions vary. Not everyone in Ireland buys the connection between social exclusion and crime, but we don't discuss it for too long. Some other issue arises, and middle-class Ireland goes back to comfortably ignoring it.

But let's return to how we spend our tax money and to our attitude towards handing our money over to the state. In 2009, just as the economy was tipping into the morass, the Revenue Commissioners commissioned a study, *A Survey on Attitudes and Behavior towards Tax and Compliance*. Now if anyone gets a phone call that includes the sentence *I'm from the Revenue and I'd like to ask you a few questions*, this might influence what the answers would be. But let's leave such cynicism aside, because the results were interesting.

The survey showed that Irish people have a pretty good understanding of what tax money is used for and that 90 per cent of us agree that paying tax is a civic duty. However, when asked if tax evasion was unacceptable, only 56 per cent of people agreed, and only 55 per cent felt that evaders should receive prison sentences. It got even more interesting when asked why people evade taxes: 68 per cent felt they were paying too much tax already, while 54 per cent felt that the taxes collected are poorly used. This second statistic in particular is another example of 'otherness' in action. We give money to some faceless body that has nothing to do with us. As we shall see later, this idea infects how we do politics in this country, but it also seems to affect our sense of morality.

The respondents were presented with 14 different anti-social behaviours – some of which involved tax, some of which didn't – and were asked to rank them in terms of unacceptableness, things like not paying a TV licence or claiming social welfare payments that you are not entitled to. Not paying taxes ranked only fourth – behind buying stolen goods, making fake social welfare claims and dropping litter on the street. Declaring some, but not all, income to the tax person came in 11th place, four places behind not paying for a ticket on public transport.

Here's the full list:

1. To drop litter on the street.
2. Deliberately claim social benefits from the Department of Social and Family Affairs that you are not entitled to.
3. To knowingly buy stolen goods.
4. To deliberately not pay the taxes you are supposed to pay.
5. To claim credits or reliefs from Revenue that you are not entitled to.
6. To drive while using a mobile phone without using a hands-free kit.

7. To use public transport (for example, buses, trains, LUAS, DART) without a valid ticket.

8. To have a TV at home without a valid TV licence.

9. To knowingly buy counterfeit goods (e.g. clothing, handbags).

10. To knowingly buy pirate goods (CDs, DVDs).

11. To declare some income but not all of your income for tax purposes.

12. To buy services knowing that the income from them will not have been declared to the tax authorities.

13. To legally avoid paying taxes by using loopholes in legislation.

14. To purchase goods abroad, and where above the limit, not declare them to Customs when they are brought into Ireland.

Clearly our attitude towards paying tax is, shall we say, nuanced, and may well have been affected by what the respondents would do themselves, given the chance, or what they may already have done. It's probably also heavily influenced by how much money they have. We are far less forgiving when other people avoid tax. Especially rich people. When it was revealed that U2 had moved part of their music empire to Holland to avoid Irish taxes, there was a blizzard of criticism, even protests at some of their gigs (in the UK). It seemed particularly – pardon the pun – *rich* for a band fronted by a man who spoke so much about poverty to be dodging taxes.

Yet U2 are not the worst offenders in this regard. There is a long list of Irish businesspeople who have decamped from this country to avoid paying tax here, while still running businesses

in Ireland. Then again, the Irish tax regime during the Celtic
Tiger was one that seemed to champion the idea that the
wealthy shouldn't have to pay much tax – that this was good
for society, because this strata of society was *good*.

The economic boom brought about the birth of a new
class in our 'classless' society: the super-stinking rich and the
socialites and various hangers-on who associated with them.
These were the people who went to the Fianna Fáil tent during
the Galway Races or had their photograph in the *Sunday
Independent* attending some swanky social do. Our politicians
fawned all over them, our media rarely criticised them and they
were allowed to present themselves to the country as patriots
– ordinary folk like you and me, really – who were doing the
best for the country. So why shouldn't the country do a bit for
them too?

The Irish are a nation known as a race with a gift for language,
with a way of piercing pomposity with a few well-chosen words.
During the Celtic Tiger years, we just seemed to lose that ability.
The crassest, most vulgar displays of wealth were served up to
us as roses we should smell. And we did. A group of people,
purely by dint of how money they had (or how much debt they
had accrued), appointed themselves the aristocracy of classless
Ireland. And nobody objected. Irony failed us.

The facts of all this are often breathtaking. There is a luxury
yacht called the *Christina O*, once owned by the fabulously
wealthy Greek shipping magnate, Aristotle Onassis. It has a
spiral staircase, a grand piano and a swimming pool that can
convert into a dance floor. JFK, Grace Kelly and Frank Sinatra
all stayed on it. In the year 2000, a company called the Christina
O Partnership, registered in the Cook Islands but comprised of

a consortium of Irish businessmen, bought it for €65 million. One of them was the developer Robert 'Pino' Harris, who then helped himself to a tax rebate from the Irish Revenue of €9.12 million because of his investment in the yacht. The Revenue did try challenging the rebate in the High Court, but lost. That's just how much our country was 'promoting business' in those days.

You can still hire out the *Christina O*. Here's the website: www. mychristinao.com. It doesn't say how much it costs (presumably if you have to ask, you can't afford it), nor does it say if Irish taxpayers get a special rate. After all, they paid for part of it.

One Irish taxpayer who did get to stay on it is the property developer Sean Dunne. He and the former *Irish Independent* columnist Gayle Killilea had their wedding reception there in 2004, reportedly at a cost of €1.5 million. The happy couple now reside in the US, where they continue to try to avoid the attentions of NAMA and the Ulster Bank. Like many Irish people, Dunne feels that he too is a victim of the financial crash. But he is also a victim of jealousy. In a 2009 interview he claimed that begrudgery was 'alive and well in Ireland'. Whoever managed to cleanse it from the Irish psyche, he suggested, should be made Taoiseach for life. His analysis was that begrudgery of winners such as himself was down to 800 years of being ruled by foreign powers. If in doubt, blame the Brits.

One person who was due to attend the Dunne/Killilea nuptials was the then Taoiseach Bertie Ahern, but he didn't make it because hanging out with zillionaires on a yacht in the Mediterranean might have sent out the wrong message to the voters. It would clash with a carefully constructed image of him as an ordinary bloke who drank pints of Bass and wore slightly shabby clothes and was forever mangling his metaphors. Four years later (at a cost of €30,000 a pop), he was giving speeches around the world on how he constructed the 'Irish economic miracle' and telling the Mahon Tribunal that for the best part of a decade he didn't have a bank account. He couldn't explain, or remember, large cash transactions (though for one he said he won the money on a horse), and eventually Mahon rejected his evidence. The questioning he faced covered the period 1988 to 1997 and involved transactions of more than £450,000 in your old punts. Depending on how you calculate it – by using the original euro-to-punt exchange rate or by adjusting it for inflation – that's between €600,000 and €880,000.

Of course, this may be down to poor money-management skills – something you wouldn't really be looking for in a former Minister for Finance. In 2003, he was forced to amend his website, which had previously claimed that he'd attended UCD and the London School of Economics. A spokesperson subsequently said, 'He has never claimed to hold degrees from UCD or anywhere else. He remembers doing the courses, but *not what they were*' (my italics). In an interview he gave in 2004, Bertie Ahern claimed he was a socialist.

Some of the people who gave Bertie Ahern money subsequently ended up on the boards of state companies, such as Aer Lingus and Dublin Port, but to this day Bertie denies that the cash had anything to do with it. He told RTÉ, 'I didn't appoint them because they gave me money. I appointed them because they were my friends.' So that's all right then.

But of course it's not. That a politician would appoint people to state boards on the basis of his friendship with them is shocking. That he *wouldn't see anything wrong with it* is where adjectives fall short. One of the many astounding aspects of the Irish economic crash is how *not one single person* in a position of power, be it in politics or banking, has taken *any* responsibility for it. The surviving Fianna Fáil politicians – because they have to – will mutter the phrase 'mistakes were made', but they are profoundly leery of being specific as to what mistakes they were. When pressed, they tend to point out that all the other parties were equally possessed by the Everything Is Awesome hysteria. Which is true, but that's far from an excuse.

Millions of words have already been written about what happened in 2008. You'll know that a heady mix of outside events, hubris, dumbness, entitlement and low morals coalesced to bankrupt the country. I'm not going to rehash all that misery. But it's worth reminding ourselves of some of the stupidity and the corruption that made it happen.

During the boom there were occasional public discussions about how all this prosperity was affecting us – that it was perhaps transforming Ireland from a society into an economy. During one such discussion on my radio show, a (presumably) young man emailed in to berate all this moaning. Detailing how he had worked hard and bought several properties, his analysis was that these 'worries' were in fact prompted by jealousy – that his generation had simply been *smarter* than those that had come before.

There was every reason for him to think that – it was the official narrative from government and from most of the media. The country appeared to be doing fabulously well, so of course it was natural to assume that it was down to something we had *done*, rather than blind luck. In 2006, a study carried out by Bank of Ireland claimed that Ireland was the second richest nation on earth, a conclusion they came to by fairly simple means. They totted up how much we all owned in investments, pensions, property and the like and came to a collective figure of close to €800 billion. They then deducted from that how much we owed to banks (€115 billion) and from that extrapolated that every woman, man and child in the state was worth €150,000. Fabulous. What they didn't stress was that three-quarters of this wealth was in property and even then many people were making noises about an overheating property market.

Yes, the world economy was doing well, but we had taken advantage of this by creating a low-tax economy that was irresistible to foreign (i.e. American) direct investment (FDI). We were English speaking and we were all so well educated. The figures bore it out. By the turn of the century we had 7 per cent of US FDI, or $38,000 for every person in the country. It was six times the EU average. We were, for a time, the largest exporter of computer software in the world. Half the manufacturing jobs in the country were from foreign companies. The economy grew and grew.

So it would have been begrudgery of the highest order to suggest that to depend so heavily on outside investment made us far too vulnerable to the global economic tides, or to point out that it hadn't made the profound difference we liked to think it had. In reality, Ireland's export in goods peaked in 2002 and steadily declined after that. In the first six years of this century, jobs in manufacturing *fell* by 20,000. But nobody noticed.

The other thing that nobody noticed was that it wasn't America providing most of the FDI; it was Holland. From 2002 on, investment from the Netherlands was always higher than that from the United States. And pretty much all of it was going to one place: the Irish Financial Services Centre (IFSC). A lot of it was actually American money belonging to corporations and routed through their Dutch treasury management subsidiaries. In 2005, around 75 per cent of all FDI in Ireland went into the IFSC. In the same year, the *New York Times* christened Dublin the 'wild west of European finance'.

The money was flowing in for two reasons: because of our low corporate tax rate and because when it came to regulation, ah, we weren't that fussed about it. As the billions flowed in, the Irish authorities were incentivised to keep the regulations nice and lax. Various publications exposed how companies had their 'head offices' in Dublin (often comprising few or no people) so they could avail of the generous tax rates. Dublin was called 'Liechtenstein on the Liffey' and outstripped the likes of the Cayman Islands as a place where the cash would be nice and safe.

The Irish government, naturally, were wounded by allegations that it was all a bit dodgy, and rather like the man who emailed my show, implied that this criticism was prompted by jealousy. Because we had been smarter.

Here's the thing: they *meant it.* Such were the tangled intersections between politicians and businesspeople, bankers and civil servants that a groupthink seemed to develop – a notion that they were all involved in a grand project to improve the country. In his book *Ship of Fools*, Fintan O'Toole writes that Fianna Fáil politicians managed to convince themselves that their close alliance with builders and developers was in fact a form of *public service.* It was all doing the country some good, even if the rules, such as they were, were getting bent. Politicians, senior civil servants and even former regulators ended up on the boards of banks and insurance companies and saw first-hand how wonderful it all was. Even at the height of the money torrent into the IFSC, some of these bankers still complained that the place was over-regulated. One person who complained about this was William Slattery, a former regulator of the IFSC.

They were all coining it, of course, but this was a generation of politicians and businesspeople who had also managed to tell themselves – and each other – that they were doing it for the most patriotic of reasons: for Ireland. And doing it in the most *Irish* of ways: by sticking it to the Other, the Other being every other country in the EU. But this was far from new, or smart. This is something we've been doing in Irish political and business culture for decades. In the 1990s, the late accountant Des Traynor was helping rich people illegally stash money in the Cayman Islands. Eventually a 10,072-page report was produced. As a result of that, 289 cases were identified. Millions of euro were recouped. No one was prosecuted. In the 1980s, the government introduced the Deposit Interest Retention Tax (DIRT), a scheme whereby banks were required to tax at source interest on deposits. The scheme, however, didn't apply to people who were non-resident in Ireland. So when it started to operate, the number of non-resident account holders suddenly tripled. By the late 1990s, 17 per cent of all deposit accounts in Ireland were 'non-resident'.

We screw Dublin, or the Tax Man, or the next county or sometimes each other.

To explain why this is, we first have to explain how politics is *supposed* to work in this country (an advance apology here: I may be about to explain the obvious).

Ireland is a representative democracy, which means we elect TDs who then go to the Dáil and Seanad to represent our interests and run the country on our behalf. New laws are proposed by the executive branch, or the Cabinet, though the 2011 coalition introduced the Economic Management Council (consisting of the Taoiseach, the Tánaiste, the Minister for Finance and the Minister for Public Expenditure and Reform), which has sucked away some of that power. Theoretically, the Executive, through the appropriate minister, presents draft legislation to the Dáil. The Dáil as a whole discusses the pros and cons and it can go through several refinements. Then it goes to the Seanad, where a similar process takes place. The Seanad can't vote it down, but it can suggest changes and send it back to the Dáil for reconsideration.

Theoretically, if any TD, government or otherwise, thinks a piece of legislation is poor or faulty or objectionable, they can vote against it, the idea being that the Oireachtas is representing the people, and if all of the Oireachtas has a say it's far more difficult for sectional interests to get laws they like or don't like passed or quashed.

But that's only theory. Realistically, such a system wouldn't get anything done. It would require convincing a majority of the 158 TDs every time a bill was put in front of them. It would be lengthy and chaotic.

That's why most parliaments have a whip system, where members of parties are instructed to vote a particular way. If they don't, they can be kicked out. But different countries apply this system in different ways. It can vary depending on the type of legislation and the custom and practice of that particular parliament.

Two examples.

In the US there is a whip system in the two houses of Congress, and while members often vote along party lines, the influence of the whip there is far weaker than in many other countries. The reason why is money. Members of Congress, in the main, raise their own money to run for office. Indeed, it's a notable feature of national US politics that fundraising is an ongoing part of their job. Thus, each politician isn't depending on their national party to get re-elected – they are paying for all that themselves.

It's also very difficult for the national party to 'de-select' a candidate, as the local support for each senator and member of Congress is so strong. Even to run for office, they've already had to go through a local primary election. For the national party to over-rule a local democratic decision is virtually impossible, especially if the politician's defiance of their national party pleases their constituency.

There's little stick and not much carrot either. Because of the sharp divisions between the Executive (the White House) and the Legislature in US politics, politicians can't be offered promotion opportunities such as ministerial positions and remain part of Congress. When John Kerry was appointed Secretary of State, for instance, he had to resign from the Senate.

As a result, the US Congress can at times be an extremely unbiddable place when it comes to getting legislation passed. Sometimes the process boils down to individual negotiations with dozens of members of Congress, each of whom wants something in return for their vote.

This system has strengths and weaknesses. The weakness is that sometimes votes are secured by what is essentially a political payoff, or what's known as an earmark. This is where a piece of legislation has a clause inserted that directs funds to something that usually has nothing to do with what the legislation is about. In 2005, for instance, $223 million was earmarked to fund the construction of a bridge from Ketchikan in Alaska to a small island called Gravina. This was attached to legislation aimed at providing reconstruction funds for New Orleans after Hurricane Katrina. The 'Bridge to Nowhere' caused a massive political stink at the time and the earmark was subsequently reversed.

The system's strength is that it gives members of Congress a direct input into the legislative process. It's not uncommon for a Republican and a Democrat to sponsor a bipartisan bill, and then go through the process of discussing it with Republican and Democrat members in the hope of winning their vote. The bill is discussed on its merits, which is the basic idea of a democratic parliament.

In the UK, the role of the government chief whip is that of enforcer but also as a conduit between the prime minister (PM) and the backbenchers. The chief whip advises the PM and the Cabinet if there is any resistance within the party to any piece of legislation. That will in turn determine what sort of whip is applied: there is a single-line whip, a double-line whip and a three-line whip. If the first two are applied and some MPs vote against, it's less of a big deal in political terms. It's a de facto recognition that not everyone will agree. If it looks like a lot of MPs are going to object, that piece of legislation may well be amended to keep the MPs happy. Again, the backbenchers can exercise some influence and have an input into the legislative process. A three-line whip is used only for what are deemed to be the most serious issues, such as votes of confidence. Defiance of a three-line whip can lead to expulsion from the parliamentary party.

In Ireland there's a three-line whip *all the time*, and as a result, your average backbencher has virtually no input into the legislative process. They are there to vote the way they are told and to turn up for the big debates so they can wave and jeer and cheer for their leaders.

The rest of the time, they work on constituency matters.

Here's how another part of our state is theoretically supposed to work. Our social services, our local authorities, our courts system, our government departments are all supposed to serve the people. They are supposed to be user-friendly. If a citizen has a problem, they should be able to get in touch quickly with the relevant person and get the answer they are looking for. But it doesn't work like that. In 2008, a report revealed that Ireland had 267 organisations with statutory powers to regulate, with 52 of them having been created in the previous four years. All these bodies, all these people, yet all too often it's the local TD who has to intercede on the citizen's behalf. And TDs get results. There's scarcely a voter in the country who hasn't had a grant or an allowance sorted out or a pothole filled because of a letter to their local deputy. And here's the thing: voters *like* this. If the politician gets you something or helps you in some way, then of course you are inclined to vote for that person again. Never mind that this is because of inefficient public services – that it encourages a degree of inefficiency – or that the country is, in effect, run by a dozen people or fewer; it's what we tend to vote for. It's one reason why TDs disgraced for corruption or tax evasion go on to top the poll the next time out. Because, like Sean Quinn, he's Our Man (it's invariably a man) and the Dublin government is the Other. When I was about 13, my uncle in Castlebar attempted to explain to me the way proportional representation works. But it wasn't about vote transfers or surpluses. He had simply drawn up a list of the candidates he was going to vote for, all of whom had done something for him or his family, apart from the last person on the list, who, he informed me, 'is a decent man'. Decency alone probably didn't get him elected.

Here's yet another paradox: most of our TDs act as advocates or quasi-social workers. It localises politics to such an extent that our national parliament isn't really national at all, but rather a meeting place for local representatives all fighting for their own areas. Yet the fact that we have such access to our politicians, that we can go meet them face to face in their constituency clinics and get their help, does humanise the way things work.

Occasionally that localism can even appear heroic. In 1982, Tony Gregory was elected as an independent TD for inner-city Dublin, a community that had been smashed to pieces by poverty, crime and a heroin epidemic. Gregory found himself holding the balance of power, so he negotiated a deal with Charlie Haughey. Haughey signed off on what would have been a £100 million rejuvenation for the area, including hundreds of new homes and thousands of jobs. In return, Gregory simply had to pledge his Dáil vote to a party and a man he would have found repellent. Some people criticised the deal for holding a government to ransom and for diverting resources at a time when the country was more broke than it is now, but most people admired what Gregory did. It was pragmatic, deal-making politics that helped a community that sorely needed it and had been neglected by the state for years.

Charlie Haughey's government didn't make it to the end of 1982 and so much of the Gregory deal was never implemented, but it was still an example of a local TD hijacking the national interest in favour of his constituents. Any other TD in the same position – and most people – would probably have done the same thing.

We ignore how the system should work in the belief that it makes it more humane. But when the system doesn't work properly we resent it and blame politicians, saying they are all in it for themselves.

Stories about civil servants abusing their position don't help either. When Limerick woman Dolores McNamara won €115 million in the EuroMillions Lottery, at least 72 officials in the Department of Social and Family Affairs were found to have looked at her file with no good reason. As punishment, each received a stern letter.

No wonder we're cynical.

Here's another comparison. In 2007 there was a massive snowstorm in New York that paralysed the airports and rendered many of the roads impassable. The storm also managed to partially bury hundreds of cars parked in Manhattan. Rather than dig them out, many of their owners decided to leave them there until the snow melted. But because of the strict parking restrictions in the city, they all got tickets. The then mayor of New York, Michael Bloomberg, decided that this was a bit harsh and decided to cancel them all. For doing so, he was slated in the press.

This wasn't politics. There was a general feeling that rules are rules, whatever the weather, and that if you park your car in Manhattan, then it's your look-out. This would never happen in Ireland. If anything, politicians would be criticised for not bending the law quickly enough.

Ireland is the living embodiment of the idea that all politics is local – a phrase most associated, appropriately, with the Irish-American politician Tip O'Neill. Now there's nothing wrong per se with TDs helping out constituents. It happens in all countries. But it becomes a problem when that's how most politicians spend most of their time – when they are not empowered to get up on their hind legs in the Dáil and ask why we had a tax system where multimillionaires could get rebates for buying luxury yachts.

After the financial meltdown in 2008 there was much public discussion about the flaws in our political system, and the general election of 2011 did seem to signal a desire for profound change.

Or did it?

In an address to the MacGill Summer School in 2014, the political editor of the *Sunday Business Post*, Pat Leahy, argued that, in fact, very little changed – and the public wanted it that way. The political *culture* of clientelism remained exactly the same. There was something of a shift to left-wing parties and independents, but very little in the way of ideological clarity from the voters. We wanted change, but we didn't know what that change was. We certainly weren't going to get any suggestions from the candidates. 'Defining what you want to change entails upsetting people,' said Leahy. 'And one of the bedrocks of Irish political culture is to avoid upsetting anyone.'

In 2011, the newly minted Taoiseach, Enda Kenny, promised a 'democratic revolution'. What we got was some minor changes to the way the Dáil does its business, a constrained Constitutional Convention that hasn't proposed any changes to the way we do politics, limits on corporate donations, a nod to gender quotas and the establishment of a Fiscal Advisory Council that has been largely ignored since it was established.

The boldest move that Fine Gael proposed was the scrapping of the Seanad, the logic being that it doesn't do much. It has an inbuilt government majority and it can't reject legislation, so why have it? Again, this wasn't change, merely the *appearance* of it. To get rid of a body that didn't have much influence would not alter how things are done in the Oireachtas. It wouldn't alter the fact that the people who clean the toilets in Dáil Éireann and backbench TDs have roughly the same amount of input into framing the laws of the state. In fact, the only change this would have brought about was the continuation of a process that has been ongoing since the foundation of the state: a creeping centralisation of power away from the Upper House and local government.

It wasn't supposed to be this way. The idea of the Seanad was that it would cast a cold eye over legislation in a chamber relatively free of party politics and bolstered by people with real-world experience. But it was never allowed to do that. Every now and again someone would point this out and the government of the day, not wishing to appear anti-democratic, would commission a report. This report would then be ignored, because to give the Seanad a real role would involve siphoning power away from the Cabinet. And no Taoiseach would ever do that.

In the history of the state, this has happened *12* times. Twelve reports on Seanad reform, 12 governments ignoring their findings and 12 elections where they were allowed to get away with it.

Another report on Seanad reform was produced in April 2015. Many commentators and politicians felt it had some positive recommendations. Few felt the government would do anything about it.

As it turned out, the 2013 referendum to junk the Seanad was rejected by the voters. And as with all such votes, every psephologist will give you a slightly different interpretation of what that vote 'meant'. It could have reflected a profound love of the Upper House or that, two years into a new government, the voters wanted to give that government a slap. There had been two further years of austerity and little sign of change. It was, perhaps, also a sign of a realisation that this mob weren't that different from the last.

Again, I risk pointing out the obvious, but *of course* they weren't different. Fianna Fáil was eviscerated in the 2011 election, and this was a dramatic change, but they were replaced by Fine Gael, a product of the same political culture and with largely the same centre-right outlook. They were locked into the same bailout programme imposed by the troika and quickly demonstrated that they weren't going to make any bold moves to reduce how much money we had to pay back.

Fianna Fáil was rightly blamed for the catastrophic mess that the country had got into. But just because Fianna Fáil had been venal and stupid didn't make the new government wise. Up until 2008, both Fine Gael and Labour were genuflecting in front of the myth of the 'Irish Economic Model' and were both fully signed up to the idea that lax banking regulations and virtually unrestrained capitalism were benefitting everyone. As late as 2007 the Labour Party was proposing tax cuts of 2 per cent and free childcare; at the time, that second proposal would have cost €1 billion a year.

In government, Fine Gael and Labour have largely followed the same economic programme as the previous coalition, have been reluctant to reform politics in any meaningful way and have proven themselves just as capable of incompetence and nepotism.

So why did we vote for them in such massive numbers? The first, and obvious, answer is that there wasn't much of an alternative at the time. The second is that the vote wasn't so much *for* FG and Labour as it was a vote *against* Fianna Fáil and the Greens. The third is that, politically, we are weirdly complacent, even lazy.

Every four years or so, Irish politicians appear on the airwaves and make a point of mentioning how sophisticated and intelligent the Irish electorate is. No one wants to question that contention. No one wants to risk being unpopular by suggesting that there's no evidence for this. What there is evidence for is that we've got the politicians and the political system we wanted – one in which the actual system is dysfunctional. Before, during and after the economic crash, poll after poll suggested that the Irish public *didn't know* what they wanted. After Bertie Ahern claimed to be a socialist in 2004, his personal approval rating went *up* by 12 per cent. In 2009, after the economic crash, he appeared on *The Late Late Show* and was warmly received by the audience. Just a few weeks before, the then Taoiseach, Brian Cowan, had also appeared on *The Late Late* and the audience did everything bar hiss at him. It was as if Bertie had nothing to do with the economic calamity and it was all Brian's fault – because Bertie was more charming.

We voted in massive numbers for the Fine Gael–Labour coalition, but a poll in 2010, just the year before, showed that most people didn't think they would do anything differently to the current government. Indeed, a majority wanted to see the late Brian Lenihan remain on as Minister for Finance – the man who was in charge on the night of the now notorious bank guarantee (and which we now know was foisted on Ireland by Europe).

The political signals the Irish voter has sent have always been confusing and contradictory, yet you'd think that when it came to the economic crash, an event made considerably worse by multiple failures of government, this would have galvanised the Irish people into some sort of action. In Greece, protests and riots became common. In France, the country was brought to a halt in 2010 by a proposal to raise the retirement age to 62. Yet we were strangely docile.

This is something that has been the subject of much analysis over the past few years and it has puzzled many. Like most things in Ireland, there isn't one overarching reason. But there are some clues.

The first is Irish fatalism. As we've said already, this runs through the Irish personality, and it was exploited massively in the years after the crash. Virtually every government politician interviewed about the economic situation would preface what they said with *The public has to know how bad things are* or a version of those words. We were pounded with the idea that there was nothing we could do about it.

Then there was the attitudinal effect of the boom. It did shift many political opinions to the right, placing Ireland, as Mary Harney once famously put it, closer to the free market ideas of Boston than the social democratic ideals of Berlin. Humans – not just Irish ones – tend to form views based at least in part on their own experience, so those who had done pretty well out of the boom (tending to be middle aged and middle class) were far less likely to protest. Instead, many of them opted to blame others for exacerbating the problem: immigrants or people on social welfare or anyone who worked in the 'cushy' public service. Others may simply have felt too guilty to make a noise. To complain that you can't afford your holiday home in Spain any more is hardly going to garner much sympathy. And chances are that the vast majority of these people did well not out of shrewdness, but blind luck. They happened to be at an age when they bought their first house (relatively) cheaply but were able to sell it for far, far more. I am one of those people. I bought my first house during the 1990s and sold it a decade later for nearly 10 times what I paid for it. Blind luck for me; the opposite for the people who bought it.

The people who were hit hardest by the crash were also the people who didn't do too well out of the boom anyway: the poor underclass. But they didn't have much in the way of political representation, and the trades union movement, traditionally where the poor and working classes have gone for help, was emasculated during the good years. Membership numbers plummeted and the social partnership arrangement helped foster the idea that they too were part of the consensus that caused the problem in the first place. So we didn't hear too much from the poor. At least at first.

There have been service cuts, all sorts of tax hikes and new charges, and on multiple occasions members of the commentariat have predicted that this would finally motivate Angry Ireland. The Universal Social Charge annoyed a lot of people, but didn't get them on the streets. There were signs of revolt against the Household Charge, but they died away too. It wasn't until 2014, six years after the financial crash, that significant numbers of people came out to protest – about water charges. This is ironic, given that the other charges were more financially onerous, yet the much-predicted 'last straw' effect does seem finally to have happened. As mentioned already, the attempt to buy off the middle classes with a smaller-than-expected charge only partially worked, and the protests have continued to be significant into 2015. Also interesting is the narrative developing among centre-left politicians and commentators that the water charges campaign has been 'hijacked' by Sinn Féin and the left. Some people are getting nervous.

Another and certainly more spectacular development was the movement that developed around garnering a Yes vote for the same-sex marriage referendum in 2015. It was a campaign almost completely devoid of politicians (we'll get to that) and one that developed from the ground up. Uniquely, it was also completely devoid of cynicism. The sight of thousands of young Irish people arriving into Dublin Airport to vote was lump-in-the-throat stuff. I don't think I've ever witnessed a political campaign with so many people crying happy tears. I know I did. On the night of the result, I went for a walk through the centre of Dublin. Around Parliament Street and Dublin Castle, the streets were clogged with people hugging and cheering. There was a real sense that everyone there had achieved something through their vote. *We* had achieved something.

In the weeks afterwards, many wondered if it would be possible to redirect this kind of political energy towards other issues, or even parliamentary politics. It's unlikely. We'll come back to that too.

Two other interesting aspects of the 2011 election were the high number of independents and a larger proportion of left-wing groups in the Dáil. The independents vary in terms of ideology, and while it does represent something of a rejection of traditional party politics, it could also be viewed as just a further strengthening of the localism of Irish political culture. But the increase of left-wing deputies, particularly those belonging to Sinn Féin, could at last be the start of something important. At the time of writing, polls indicate that Sinn Féin could end up as one of the largest parties in the Dáil. Add to that the emergence of the centre-right Renua Ireland, and we might – just might – be starting to see the arrival of left–right politics in this country, and with it the end of the fantasy that we don't have a class system. Of course, we don't know yet how this might affect the way we do politics, if at all. That would require a demand from the public far beyond simple rage about the water charges. The polls also indicate that independents will be returned in large numbers. So it's just as likely that we might end up with political chaos. Or nothing might happen. In March 2015 there were signs that the Fine Gael–Labour coalition was starting to get a rise in the polls, due mainly to an improvement in the economy. Distracted by the financial grind of the last few years, politics becomes all about the economy, and the wider concerns are forgotten. As the philosopher Hegel said, 'We learn from history that we learn nothing from history.'

There is more to politics in Ireland than just the economic crash. But first we should have a look at the media. They were hardly impartial observers in all this. They reported on what was happening, arguably made it worse and certainly didn't pay enough attention to signs that things were about to go horribly wrong. In 2014, UCD academic Julien Mercille published *The Political Economy and Media Coverage of the European Economic Crisis: The Case of Ireland.* Not the snappiest title, admittedly, but it was a serious look at how the media (though he concentrated on print for the book) reported the boom, the bust and all that lovely property porn. Mercille basically pored through the newspapers over a number of years and was able to come up with statistical evidence that the papers presented overwhelmingly pro-boom, pro-building coverage. He subsequently told the Oireachtas banking inquiry that 'a number of journalists simply acted as cheerleaders for the property sector'.

He also told the inquiry that this had happened for three reasons: close ties with corporate and government interests, reliance on advertising and the sourcing of stories. These reasons are probably more inferences on his part than rock-solid proof, but they are worth considering.

It depends on what you mean by 'close ties', but it is the case that your average political correspondent will spend much of their time within the bubble of the Oireachtas, and it's human nature that they might get caught up in the internecine squabbles that sometimes pass for politics there. They'll cultivate sources for stories, but to get a story usually involves some degree of horse-trading. No TD will leak information to a journalist just for the sake of it. They will have their own reasons for doing so, and when the journalist publishes that story, they have become, inevitably, part of the political process. Similarly, journalists start to like some politicians more than others and of course will have their own political opinions. In a job where they are under constant pressure to meet a variety of deadlines, they have to question their own motives to make sure they are being fair. They also have to guess the motives of TDS who give them information. Because of the constant time constraints – exacerbated by the modern requirement not only to file copy but also to record a podcast, make a short video clip and write three blogs – they are limited in how many sources they can go to when researching a story. It's incredibly difficult to get right; actually, it's *impossible* to get right.

I work in the media, so of course this is bound to influence my opinion on it, but I do feel that the vast majority of political journalists try to be as fair and impartial as possible. They take their job seriously. Having said that, I think it's fair to say that most media organs in Ireland are, politically, centre or centre-right. They tend to be liberal on social issues (such as same-sex marriage, for instance) and to support the current structure of our economy. This isn't an explicit bias, but it can be detected in the assumptions behind how stories are reported and presented. Business journalists, for instance, will invariably report on new business developments as a good thing, and that's because every day they are interviewing people in the business world who would think similarly. Business journalists don't tend to be socialists, and there should be no great surprise in that. In sourcing their stories, they are even more restricted. It's basically businesspeople (or their PR representatives), all of whom would have a particular view of the economy and how it should be organised.

It can also be argued, correctly, that the inclination of the media reflects the general inclination of society. Look at the make-up of the Dáil, and it's dominated by centre and centre-right parties.

However, it's not the job of the media *just* to simply reflect back to people what they think already. Part of it should also involve, in my opinion, introducing new ideas, different ways of looking at our society – of organising things. Many of those ideas might turn out to be wrong – they probably will – but to consider an alternative at the very least makes us examine how we are doing things now. And most people would agree that the way we organise our state now is far from perfect.

So in this, Mercille would appear to be correct. Here's one example. Based on the make-up of the Dáil in early 2015, around 15 per cent of the TDs (Sinn Féin, United Left Alliance and other independents) could be described as left wing. Thus, at least 15 per cent *of the country* would hold a similar point of view. Is 15 per cent of our media left leaning? It's a rhetorical question; you don't need to answer.

The media doesn't completely ignore the need for diversity of opinion, be it from the left or right. There's Gene Kerrigan, Ian O'Doherty, Kevin Myers, Vincent Browne. It was the *Irish Times* that published Morgan Kelly's article in 2006 that predicted the property crash. But these are notable exceptions. All too often the Irish media runs the risk of a milky complacency, bordering on smugness.

Mercille's second contention – that reliance on advertising affected the tone of reporting – I simply don't buy. Certainly property porn helped fuel the boom, and perhaps journalists regarded the existence of all that advertising as evidence that all was well, but that's distinctly different from an explicit or implicit threat that unfavourable coverage of events would cause advertising to go elsewhere.

Admittedly, I base this simply on my own experience. I've worked in the media for 30 years and I've never come across a situation where advertising had any influence over editorial content. Indeed, the usual situation in most media organisations is that editorial and advertising exist in an uneasy alliance, each feeling the other doesn't appreciate how important they are. Journalists are rarely guilty of not taking themselves seriously enough and would be anything but biddable in response to any attempt to influence their work. Most would regard such stubbornness as a source of pride.

For their part, the editors who appeared before the banking inquiry all vehemently denied that advertising played any part in influencing content. But for them to say it – for me to say it – simply isn't good enough. That there is a suspicion at all represents a failure, one fuelled not just by the events of the boom and crash, but by how economics has affected the media business.

Up until the 1990s, media in Ireland (at least the print media) was much more varied. It was economically feasible – just about – to produce publications containing high-quality journalism that might challenge what you read elsewhere. When I started as a journalist, there was the likes of *Magill*, *In Dublin* (at its best) and *Hibernia*. But for various reasons, they all fell away. It became increasingly difficult for the small independent publication to survive, and the arrival of the internet made it impossible.

It also put pressure on the larger mainstream publications, with the result that many of them shelter within the relative protection of larger media groups. Landmark Media, controlled by the Crosbie family, owns a dozen newspaper titles, including the *Irish Examiner* and a number of radio stations and websites. Independent News and Media has interests in 22 countries, including five national Irish titles and 14 regional titles. UTV Radio owns seven locals stations on the southern side of the border. In turn, 29 per cent of Independent News and Media is owned by Denis O'Brien, who also owns Communicorp, which owns five radio stations in Ireland and dozens of others around the world. This includes Newstalk, the station I work for.

There's nothing wrong with large media companies and there are limits on media ownership in Ireland; the rules did prompt Communicorp to sell FM104. But the very fact of this large ownership and the corporate culture that comes with it does tend to drown out the independent voices. And there's always the tang of suspicion that, editorially, they are centrally controlled. I have worked in Newstalk for 10 years and in that time I've met Denis O'Brien perhaps three times, for about 30 seconds on each occasion. It was a handshake and hello. In my decade there, no one has ever told me I could or couldn't say anything. Yet I am regularly forced to point this out to texters or people on Twitter who suspect otherwise. It's not always a comfortable position to be in.

But back to Mercille. His final point is correct. The Irish media reported that everything was rosy with the boom, and that's because everyone the media spoke to parroted the same message, including the vast majority of economists. With a few notable exceptions, *everyone* got it wrong. The media reported the positive news it got from 'experts' and politicians, who read the positive news and fed it back to the media. It was a feedback loop of delusional bullshit, so much so that when Morgan Kelly's article was published in the *Irish Times*, the *Sunday Independent* attacked him for 'tabloid economics' – and the reaction from the vast majority of 'expert' columnists was pallid at best, as if they couldn't quite believe this was happening. Hundreds of thousands of Irish people used this reportage as the basis on which to make profound financial decisions – to buy homes, to take out more bank loans – and the media was misinforming them. It may have been inadvertent – like most people, the media was lulled by groupthink – but there was a failure to give time and space to the contrary view, to those who didn't buy into the orthodoxy or weren't part of an elite. The Irish media has been slow to take responsibility for this.

Like most of the western world, Irish media culture lionises entrepreneurism and employs meaningless terms like *solutions* (an aside: not too long ago I had dealings with a person whose job title was Head of Solutions and Insight – something to do with the internet, apparently). But the most abused word is *innovation*. In the vast majority of situations, what is presented as innovation is in fact the same thing in different packaging: marketing. Human nature is such that people are fearful of and uncomfortable around profound change. Politicians certainly don't like it and the media doesn't like it either. Because it has to, the media is struggling to figure out how to deal with the World Wide Web. But what it doesn't seem to have considered at all is *how* it reports news and how it explores issues, or if the way it is done now is as socially useful as it could be.

To be fair, this is something that affects media all over the world. And admittedly, I am in a tiny minority on this one. But I do feel that much of our reporting of politics is more pageant than sober exploration. It's more to do with getting the audience to *feel* a certain way than getting them to *think*.

Here's an example. Your standard political interview on radio or TV is called a 2+1: the interviewer plus two people with opposing points of view on a particular issue. Theoretically, what's supposed to happen is a watered-down version of the philosophical idea of a dialectic: one person proposes an idea and the other critiques it, the hope being that the idea could be improved or that a new, better idea might emerge.

But of course nothing like that happens, *ever*. Both the politicians have had their media training. The interviewer will be keen to appear equally tough on both. The last thing anyone wants is any thoughtful or socially useful examination of the issue ostensibly being discussed. The politicians will avoid the questions where they appear 'weak' and will have a pre-prepared set of points on which to attack the other politician, most of which have nothing to do with the issue at hand ('I won't be lectured by a party that …' etc. etc.).

The whole point of the exercise is to emerge from it *looking good*. The viewer or listener usually learns nothing new, or comes away from it not having had their attitudes even mildly challenged. And they don't want to. These kinds of media exchanges are more like sporting events. The audience members support one side or the other and they tune in not to learn, but in the hope of seeing one of the politicians humiliated or made to seem uncomfortable. It's pugilistic entertainment, not journalism. If the audience makes a judgement at all, it's on how the politician performed in the interview, not if the policy is a good or bad one or if the politician is good or bad at their job. And this contributes to the cynicism of the process. The politician turns up prepared not to be honest because that equates to weakness and will be exploited by the media. The audience sees politicians not answering questions, which in turn confirms their cynicism about politicians. We have a political culture where politicians are punished for telling the truth. So they don't.

Now this is not to say that there aren't many fine journalists on radio and television in Ireland. There obviously are. The standard in this country is as good as anywhere in the world, and in many cases better. And there have been instances where an interview has revealed the nonsensical nature of a particular policy – Marian Finucane's 2001 interview with Joe Jacob on how the government would cope with a problem in Sellafield is a classic example – but they are notable for their rarity.

The effect of this system is to set politicians and the media permanently at loggerheads. The book *Political Communication in the Republic of Ireland*, edited by Mark O'Brien and Donnacha Ó Beacháin, describes in some detail just how many ministers and party leaders go out of their way to *not* communicate with journalists, such is their sense that anything they say will be reported negatively. In his 11 years as Taoiseach, Bertie Ahern never briefed political correspondents in the Dáil, limiting his contact to being doorstepped as he travelled from one meeting to another. That way he could keep his comments short and inconsequential while also giving the impression that he was a terribly busy man but one who wasn't so up himself that he didn't have time for a brief chat with his friends in the press. Genius.

Politics, though, is about more than just how the Oireachtas is organised or who's to blame for the country going bust. There are a few other issues that come back to hit us every now again, even though we might like them to go away.

Abortion. How conscientious are we about abortion?

You don't need me to tell you how, on occasion, the country has become a pretty horrible place when the issue has come up for discussion. We will be talking about Irish neuroticism later on, but Irish debates about abortion have been an exercise in self-loathing. We have tried to face in two directions at the same time and it simply hasn't worked.

The whole mess started in 1983 when the Fine Gael–Labour coalition was effectively bullied into introducing an amendment to the Constitution to ban abortion. Pro-life groups had worried that another clause in the Constitution, guaranteeing 'privacy in marital affairs', could be construed at some later date as allowing abortion. After a nasty and fractious campaign, the amendment passed. In the argument over how the amendment should be worded, many had pointed out that there are situations where an abortion is medically necessary – that to give birth would kill the mother. Thus, the wording also gave 'equal regard to the right to life of the mother'.

Less than a decade later, the x Case happened. A 14-year-old girl, raped by a friend of her family, was denied permission by the Attorney General to travel to the UK for a termination. It was grotesquely cruel, and one of those rare occasions when Irish society as a whole seemed to shudder at the realisation of what it had done. On appeal, this decision was reversed, and later that year Ireland voted to legalise the right to travel for abortion and the right to get information about it in advance.

The x Case also established a legal precedent, whereby the threat of suicide also became grounds to have a legal termination in Ireland. On two occasions, Irish governments have tried to get rid of this precedent through changes to the Constitution. The Irish electorate rejected it both times.

With such a clear signal, you'd think Irish politicians would accept it and usher through the necessary legislation. But they didn't do this until 2013 – 21 years after the x Case, and after a woman had died in an Irish hospital.

So here's the legal situation. Obviously, abortion is illegal in Ireland except when there's a risk to the life (as opposed to the health) of the mother, including a risk from suicide.

In the case of physical risk, the termination must be signed off by two doctors. If there's a threat of suicide, the distressed woman must be examined – in succession – by two psychiatrists and an obstetrician, and again, all must agree that the threat is real.

It is legal for a woman to travel outside the state for an abortion (in 2010, 3,500 women gave Irish addresses to UK clinics) and Irish doctors are required to provide follow-up care. Contact details can be provided by Irish doctors or counsellors, though they must not specifically advocate for an abortion or even contact the clinic on the woman's behalf. In the case of lethal foetal abnormality – if it's pretty clear the baby will not survive outside the womb – abortion is still illegal. Women are required to go to full term. In the case of rape or incest, abortion is also illegal.

The decision to legislate for the x Case came after the death of Savita Halappanavar in a Galway hospital. Seriously ill, she had repeatedly asked for a termination and had been refused. An inquiry afterwards found that the hospital hadn't dealt properly with her symptoms and concluded that the fault was medical, not because of confusion surrounding the legal situation. On the face of it, her death actually had nothing to do with the failure to legislate for x. Yet it still prompted marches and revived the sense that has billowed through Irish society regularly over the past few decades that we had once again failed a woman in dire need.

Due to other court cases that had been taken since 1992, successive governments had been under increasing pressure to finally legislate. So they did.

The question is: why did it take so long?

On two occasions, the public had voted to retain the threat of suicide as a basis for legal termination. Repeated polls, going back over 10 years, have shown consistent support for legislating for the x Case. Not only that, but there has been growing support for liberalising the rules. An *Irish Times* poll in October 2014 found 68 per cent of people in favour of allowing abortion in cases of rape, incest or if the foetus was not viable outside the womb. A *Sunday Independent* poll in September of the same year found that 56 per cent of people were in favour of scrapping the original 1983 amendment altogether. A poll by the same paper in April 2015 found the figure had swelled to almost two-thirds. Many of the people who marched after the death of Savita had never done so before. A new generation became politicised, at least in terms of this issue, and on social media at least there is a proto-movement to repeal the Eighth Amendment.

But experience tells us that it will take far more than a couple of polls and a hashtag to get the political class to move on this, because their reluctance to move quickly, or at all, is also based on experience.

The pro-life movement in Ireland might be relatively small, but it is extremely well organised. Certainly whenever the issue of abortion comes up on my radio show we tend to get a flurry of emails in, all arguing against abortion, all from people who claim not to be members of any group, but whose emails all have suspiciously similar wording. In the run-up to the vote on the Protection of Life During Pregnancy Bill in 2013, they piled on the pressure. Every TD I interviewed told me that their inbox was crammed with missives imploring them not to vote. Some were from self-identified groups, some were from individuals. Many were abusive. Others were threatening.

In public debates, they employed a strategy that's been used in Ireland for decades. It's been used for abortion and, before that, for divorce and contraception, the basic narrative being that if you legalise this thing, the public will go mad using it. Contraception was supposed to usher in a tidal wave of promiscuity. Divorce would bring with it marital breakdown on a massive scale, and the legalising of abortion, even to this faint degree, would encourage women to pretend to be suicidal.

Written down, such an argument might seem daft, but it is enough to put doubt in the minds of some voters, and in turn to spook some TDs. Even though the bill passed comfortably, Enda Kenny set his face against a free vote, the reason being that it would provide political cover to some of his nervous TDs – they could go back to their constituents and argue that the party whip made them do it. And those TDs were nervous for a very good reason: because they know their constituents. Despite the referendum results, despite the polls, despite the old cliché that 'the public are ahead of the politicians on this one', TDs know that when it comes down to it, many Irish people are flaky on abortion. In the days after the latest tragedy they might be sympathetic to pollsters, but months later, when it's time to make a difficult, sober decision, they are not so sure. We blame politicians for a lot, but we voted for them. Even while they are annoying us, they are also reflecting back who we are.

In the event, four Fine Gael TDs voted against the bill and were promptly expelled from the parliamentary party, which for Fine Gael was limited damage. As a political strategy, the Taoiseach was right to enforce the whip. Many papers at the time had been speculating that as many as 10 of his own TDs might rebel. In fairness, this wasn't just all down to self-interested electoral concerns. TDs are Irish people too and are entitled to their opinions.

This is also why, despite numerous polls giving a high margin to the Yes side – and the subsequent massive Yes vote – many government TDs quietly stayed out of the way when it came to the 2015 referendum on same-sex marriage. But that's putting it mildly. Only a handful of TDs from *any* of the political parties campaigned. Within Fianna Fáil, it was down to the TD Pat Carey (who had revealed he was gay some months before) and Senator Averil Power. The *Irish Times* reported that when Power asked her parliamentary party colleagues for help with campaigning, she was laughed at. TDS are entitled to their opinions, but that doesn't inoculate them from stupidity. Two days after the result, Power resigned from Fianna Fail.

Of course, I have argued all this from a particular point of view, for which, as many TDS are fond of saying, I make no apology. But even the most avidly anti-abortion person could not be happy with this situation either. The lack of clarity is in no one's interest, and certainly not in the interest of women. The political skittishness around abortion is borne out of fear, but it's also a reflection of how Ireland, as a supposedly grown-up country, has yet to make up its mind. We don't seem to want to. Unlike pretty much any other public issue, it's difficult to come to an emphatic conclusion on what to do, because for the vast majority of women, an abortion is not something to be undertaken lightly. It is an option taken when the other options are even worse. It is uncomfortable, morally grey and often sad. And unless it affects us personally, we don't seem to want to think about it. Because after all, in the vast majority of cases, it's something that happens to Other People.

After the massive Yes vote in the same-sex marriage referendum, there were many suggesting that perhaps the Yes movement could now be deployed to campaign for the repeal of the Eighth Amendment. But that's unlikely to happen. Sadly, the same-sex marriage campaign was probably a one-off. It was built around a simple and extremely positive proposition: for the state to recognise the love of LGBT people. Part of the campaign was a celebration of love. It was easy to take a black-and-white view. It's far more difficult when it comes to most other issues, but particularly that of abortion.

Almost certainly, there will be a campaign to repeal the Eighth Amendment. The Labour Party and Amnesty International have already committed to campaigning. But it's likely to be nasty and brutish political trench warfare. It has to be done, but no one will relish the prospect.

Something else we don't tend to think about much – and something that other people do – is the Irish language. I was 12 when we moved to Ireland so I didn't have to do it at school (for all her fierceness in insisting I was Irish, my mother was equally fierce in making sure I didn't have to learn the language). But in my first year in school in Ireland, and because there was nowhere else to put me, I had to sit at the back of Irish class and 'study' while all the others droned phlegmy-sounding phrases shouted at them by a tweedy teacher. Most of the time I had no idea what anyone was saying, and most of the time, neither did any of the others. The air of boredom, even despair, lay thick in the room – learning by rote about long-dead people living in parts of the country that had long since been concreted over. During that first year, the phrase I heard most often was: *You don't have to do Irish. You're so lucky.*

That the language has been taught in schools in the most unattractive way has been a much-ventilated subject, and it certainly has been a factor in the demise of its use. But it's surely not the only factor.

Language is one of the major ways in which nations are different to each other – not just in the way they sound, but in the way they view the world. Different languages are constructed in different ways and offer differing methods of describing emotions, thoughts and the physical world. Language has a direct effect on how we *think*. Even though Irish is now spoken by only a tiny percentage of the population, it still influences us in our use of English, and thus in the way we view the world. At least some of the English dialect we speak – Hiberno-English – came about by translating phrases from Irish, which is why our version of English tends to be more courtly and playful. Hiberno-English has also retained some words from Old and Middle English that are not used in any other part of the world any more. *Ye* is still used as a plural of *you*. *Yoke* is a word borrowed from Middle English that's unique to us.

However, because of globalisation, television, the internet and other factors we've discussed already, the situation is changing. Hiberno-English has been spoken here since the 12th century and Irish is one of the oldest vernacular languages in Europe – and these inter-linked tongues are *both* are under threat.

We love the Irish language, at least in theory. A 2009 study by Micheál Mac Gréil found that 93 per cent of people have positive aspirations for the language, ranging from reviving it across the country (40 per cent) to seeing it preserved in Gaeltacht areas (52 per cent). Only 7 per cent felt it should be discarded, though for some reason the highest proportion of people who felt this way were in their 70s.

The survey also found that 9 per cent considered themselves to be fluent and that over 10 per cent use the language on at least a weekly basis.

Which all sounds great. But if it were true you'd be hearing Irish being spoken all the time. And you don't. Using the language on a weekly basis might just involve saying *slán* occasionally, and fluency can be a very subjective measure.

The modern reality is that the use of Irish even in Gaeltacht areas has shrunk dramatically. A 2003 study claimed that it is in daily use by only 25 per cent of the people who live there. A 2007 study found that the actual Gaeltacht was much smaller than the officially designated area – that it had shrunk to three enclaves in Donegal, Galway and Kerry. Many claim that children growing up in Gaeltacht areas, even if they live in an Irish-speaking house, are more proficient in English than Irish.

Elsewhere there is evidence of people actively ignoring it. In 2010, out of the 55,000 people sitting the Leaving Certificate, more than 4 per cent had claimed an exemption from taking Irish on the basis of a learning disability. Yet half of those people had miraculously overcome the disability to take French, German or Spanish. Indeed, there don't seem to be any reliable figures on how many people speak Irish as a first language. The guestimates are that it could be between 20,000 and 40,000. More people in Ireland speak Polish.

The lip service (pardon the pun) that most Irish people give to the first official language is once again reflected back at us by our parliament. In 2004 the government passed the Official Languages Act, the idea being that over time all government services could be provided through Irish. This led to lots of money being spent on documents and signs being translated into Irish. There was even a *Coimisinéir Teanga* – or Language Commissioner – appointed to make sure the process ran smoothly. After 10 years in the job he resigned, claiming that a lot of the changes hadn't been implemented. And anyway, it was starting to look a lot like tokenism. Having bilingual signs and documents doesn't make people speak more Irish. It just makes it *look* that way.

Study after study has looked at the decline of Irish in Gaeltacht areas, and all have come to the same conclusion: that from the 1960s on, there has been a steady immigrant stream of people for whom Irish was not a first language, or a language at all. This has changed the socio-linguistic balance in the areas so that people, particularly young people, now tend to speak English first among their peers. Add to that other factors that also threaten Hiberno-English – the internet and the global, American-speaking media – and Irish faces the same threat as up to 90 per cent of the world's languages: it will be extinct by the end of this century.

Perhaps *extinct* is too strong a word. It will live on as a subject for academic study. There will be some literature. There will still be speakers who will come together. But as a living tongue – where ordinary people say *Conas atá tú?* on the street – it faces an existential threat. Despite the pieties we utter, the chances of Irish becoming a language spoken or even part-spoken by most people are remote, and they are zero if the Irish-speaking areas are allowed to die.

They can be saved, even grown into sustainable communities. It would take a lot of political will and a lot of money. Ultimately, it depends on how much we, as a society, value them. But if you were to judge us by our actions so far, the answer is: not much.

But perhaps even more important than saving the language is reunifying the country. Or is it? An admission about this book: it's about the Irish, but by that I mean people who live in the Republic of Ireland. I simply don't know enough about the North even to attempt to make any judgements about the people who live there. They seem different.

Of course they are different. Since the foundation of this state the experiences of people in the Republic and Northern Ireland have been wildly different. The dynamics of the two societies have been different, and over the years a gulf of ignorance and (in the Republic) a degree of indifference has grown up. That's not to say that the South wouldn't like a united Ireland. Repeated polls have indicated that this is the case, though the figures have hardly been overwhelming. A *Sunday Independent* survey in 2005 found 55 per cent in favour, though half of them said they would not be prepared to pay any more taxes to get it (given the state of the Northern Ireland economy, that would be a virtual certainty). In 2010, a *Sunday Times* poll pushed the figure up to 57 per cent. A survey by the *Sunday Business Post* in 2006 did come out with an 80 per cent majority in favour of reunification, but of that figure, 55 per cent said it should not be 'the first priority of government'. Summing up his view of political opinion in the Republic, the late political scientist Peter Mair once wrote, 'Unity would be nice. But if it's going to cost money, or result in violence, or disrupt the moral and social equilibrium, then it's not worth it.'

Rather tellingly, during the RTÉ *Frontline* television debate for the presidential election of 2011, a member of the audience said to the Sinn Féin candidate, Martin McGuinness, 'I am curious as to why you have come down here to *this* country.' McGuinness got 13.7 per cent of the first preference votes. However, as he isn't normally resident in the Republic, he wasn't eligible to vote for himself.

In the past few years it's become a standard features idea for the media to find people who have never crossed the border before to visit the other part of the island and see what they think, which in itself speaks volumes about the differences in the two societies. The *Irish Times* did it in 2014, and while it was easy to find people in the Republic who had never been to the North, it took weeks to find Northerners who had never been to the Republic. This is an odd imbalance. In 2013, Northerners made 1.6 million trips to the Republic during which they stayed for at least one night. Southerners made only 400,000 such trips. We made 50 per cent more trips to France and 150 per cent more trips to Spain.

Even politicians acknowledge that there are differences. Since 2014, Micheál Martin, the leader of the Republican party, Fianna Fáil, has been pushing a notably softer line on unification. Now it's 'a genuine unity of people who can work in harmony, meet in harmony, engage in harmony and break down the barriers … a unity of people rather than a unity of territory'. Whatever that means.

It's likely that this has been prompted by his sense that it's not high on the political agenda in the Republic or even in the North. A BBC *Spotlight* poll in 2013 found 65 per cent of people opposed to a united Ireland, and that included 38 per cent of Catholics.

A poll in 2005 in Northern Ireland reported similar results, but also some interesting attitudes on other matters. Eighty-two per cent felt that religion will 'always make a difference' in Northern Ireland, 42 per cent felt that sex before marriage was wrong and 63 per cent were opposed to homosexuality. In the now secular South, we easily forget how much religion – particularly the fundamentalist Bible-bashing kind – is still deeply ingrained in the culture. In the final decade or so of his life, Ian Paisley may have pushed a kinder image of himself, but he still promoted a version of Protestantism that was weirdly obsessed with the Roman Catholic Church and 'the Vatican conspiracy to overthrow civil government from the 12th century to the present'.

Of course, we can't afford to be that smug about such things. For many years the Republic was a Catholic country with a big c. We were an insular, backward state where our elected representatives were happy to take their guidance from the bishops. The writer Jason Walsh, who is from the North, makes the intriguing point that partition effectively created two states, both of which were overly defined by religion. If partition had never happened, we might have been forced to create a society based on more liberal secular values.

But the main difference, of course, has been the years of violence. Over those years, opinion in the Republic has wobbled between sympathy, sneaking regard, disgust, shame and bafflement. But since the Good Friday Agreement, it's been mostly bafflement. The arrival of peace (or the absence of war) has allowed the Republic to largely forget about the six counties – to assume that that nagging problem has finally been resolved – allowing the rest of us to get on with the proper grown-up business of developing a booming economy. Since the 1990s, all that's been reported about the North is disputes about marches and flags, occasional riots and occasional bursts of violence from people who seemed to live not just in a different country, but in a different century.

So it's always interesting to see the reaction to politicians from the North when they arrive down here. The political necessities of Northern Ireland required Martin McGuinness to admit his involvement in the IRA. But the reverse seems to be the case in this part of the island. Gerry Adams, while not 'disassociating' himself from the IRA, has consistently claimed that he was not a member. Many others, both from inside and outside the Republican movement, dispute this. But perhaps in the South we require such ambivalence. Part of the price for peace in Northern Ireland is the stomach-churning reality that people who have carried out appalling acts get to walk the streets there now. Members of the family of Jean McConville, who was kidnapped and shot dead by the IRA in 1972, have reported getting taxis in Belfast where the driver was one of the people who abducted their mother. We certainly don't want that kind of thing down here, and certainly not in our elected representatives.

But here's the thing: given that he is 'associated' with the IRA, Gerry Adams is 'associated' with some appalling acts of butchery, both in the North and in the Republic. There are few other Irish politicians you could say that about. Yet he is a man who also risked his own life for the peace process. For many years he conducted secret talks and had to dance around the truth with the aim of convincing the IRA to decommission. At any point during this process, people from his own side, had they discovered what he was up to, could easily have construed such actions as betrayal and put a bullet in his head. Whatever about what other activities he may or may not have been involved in, that took courage. There are few other Irish politicians you could say that about either.

Perhaps all those years of secrets and risk don't equip a person for the more humdrum politics of the Republic, where our primary concerns are about euros and cents, not national determination. He's been criticised for not being a great Dáil performer and for not being greatly informed about 'Southern' issues, though observers say he has improved.

He's also a bit of an odd fish. I've interviewed him a couple of times, and on the second occasion he told me (and the audience present) that he likes to bounce naked on a trampoline. Sometimes a dog joins in. He was probably joking, but in that deadpan, *Northern* way, you can never be sure. After the interview was over, he shook my hand and said, 'Happy Valentine's Day.' I've no idea what he meant by that.

Under his leadership, Sinn Féin has done fantastically well in the Republic in a very short space of time. The party has a firm, largely working-class base of support. But to expand that into the middle classes will be difficult. That ambivalence, that whiff of danger, would have to be completely eradicated. That will take a while.

Perhaps there will be a united Ireland, but it doesn't seem as if it will be any time soon. The more the Republic boomed and became more pleased with itself, the more Northern Ireland seemed like a dysfunctional backwater, filled with bitter people obsessed with the petty demands of their religious and political gods. We wished the North well, of course. We even wished for a united Ireland. But not yet – not like this. From middle-class Ireland there has been an underlying sense that we'd like to unify, but only when the people there are more like us.

Chapter 5

Postmodern
Meta-slagging:
Are We Neurotic?

When I was a kid in Ballinasloe, out of the gaudy sweetshop of insults available to young men, one of the most popular was *he thinks he's fucking great*. Not exactly Oscar Wilde, but its power lay in the myriad inferences that could be drawn from those five words. By thinking you're great, you think you're better than everyone else, which clearly you are not, given that this insult has been hurled at you. Which means you are slightly delusional – you have an inflated sense of self based on attributes you do not possess. And in the microscopic community of teenage Ballinasloe, this is bound to have been noticed. If one person thinks this of you, then possibly *everyone* thinks the same. Everyone has been secretly laughing at your puffed-up egomania, even the people you thought were your friends. You are not part of this community. They look down on you. You're not great. You're alone.

Ouch.

You may be wondering, so yes, sometimes this insult was thrown at me. Luckily, I was protected by a near-invulnerable cloak of teenage cockiness and by my English literalism. I took the words at face value and they made no sense to me. Why *wouldn't* you think you are great? Shouldn't everyone? Are you supposed to think you are mediocre? Is that what you should aim for?

It took me many more years to understand the nuances of Hiberno-English, insofar as I do. The sting of a phrase like that can vary depending on the tone used, the situation and the person saying it. But *you think you're great* is predicated on the idea of the unacceptability not of greatness, but of *difference.* In small communities, in small countries, different is viewed with suspicion. Social cohesion seems to be tied up with the notion that everyone should be more or less the same. Thinking you're great may also come with an implied judgement – that everyone else *isn't* great.

This kind of tall poppy syndrome – or begrudgery – is not unique to Ireland, but mix it up with fatalism, the inferiority complex we talked about earlier, a deep strain of melancholy in Irish culture and our astonishing ability to talk a lot but not say anything, and you get a unique stew of Irish emotional dysfunction. At times, it would drive you mad. All too often, it does drive us mad. Literally.

We have ambivalent feelings towards all these national characteristics. We regularly flail ourselves for begrudgery, yet we celebrate it too. Even though the word *begrudge* is used elsewhere, the term *begrudgery* is unique to Ireland. We all assume there's lots of it and that it has a corrosive effect on how we view our society and each other, yet it's trickier to pin down than you might think. In public, incidents of begrudgery are only ever pointed out by the people who feel they are subject to it. No one ever *admits* to being a begrudger; indeed, they will defend their attitude as fair comment. On a recent Reddit thread, one poster recalled Bono's 2002 interview with Oprah Winfrey during which he decried Irish begrudgery. The Reddit contributor wrote, 'I don't begrudge Bono his success. I just think he's a wanker.'

Slagging off celebrities is something pretty much all Irish people enjoy, and with good reason – many of our public figures do come across as pompous twits with little self-awareness. To use that beautiful, damning Irish phrase, they have *notions about themselves.* They are no better than the rest of us, but they've forgotten it. They've forgotten that it's far from Pinot Grigio they were raised. The beauty of media culture is that we never learn any more about them than the largely two-dimensional image we get. It's easy to think Bono is a wanker if all we have to go on are the ubiquitous v-signs and a few sound bites, but it might be more difficult if you saw him at home with his kids. We can fill in the blank bits and make all sorts of assumptions and never be troubled that we might be proven wrong. In my years at Newstalk I've often been astonished at the level of abuse that comes in for some of the guests I interview, especially the ones who work in entertainment or showbiz. Compared to the bankers or politicians who actually damaged the country, they're harmless.

Case in point. A few times a year we have Amanda Brunker on the show. She is funny and honest and one of those people who always has some project on the go. Over the last 20 years she's been Miss Ireland, had a long-running newspaper column, acted, written novels, written plays and presented TV shows. Briefly (and unwisely) she attempted to be a singer. She is, or was, one of those people always getting their photograph taken in some nightspot. She has said a few stupid things over the years. She's friends with Bono (not showbiz friends – their families were neighbours) and perhaps mentions that a bit too much. But she's smart and a hard worker. She doesn't take herself too seriously, and unlike many people in the media, she knows she's only as good as her last gig.

But every time she's on with us, the naked hatred she receives from some of the listeners is astounding. This comes via texts and Twitter, from men and women. There are lots of adjectives. *Stupid* is a common one, and among the mildest. I have on occasion tried to engage with some of these people on Twitter, and a few of them, after some thought, were unable to explain why they had reacted to her so badly. In fact, it didn't seem to be about *Amanda Brunker* at all, but what she represented to them. That she was a former beauty queen. That she knows Bono. That she's a *sort* of person – a member of a stratum in society who have it easy: people who think they're great.

This, however, doesn't feel like *just* begrudgery, but something else too, like she's an avatar for all sorts of resentments and ideas that her critics are only half aware of. As though hating her – a person they don't actually know – is almost a form of therapy.

Admittedly, I'm guessing here. They could just think she's a wanker too.

Then again, many of the people who complain about begrudgery are people who, one could argue, deserve criticism, or at least to have a bit of fun poked at them. Sean Dunne and Sean Quinn both moaned about it, and so did huge swathes of the conquer-the-world business community when it seemed the rest of us didn't sufficiently appreciate their messianic awesomeness (whoops! was that begrudging?). When the crash came and a lot of them were in NAMA or hiding in foreign jurisdictions, they complained even more. Politicians complain about it, especially when (according to them) it comes from other politicians. Indeed, the charge of begrudgery is the go-to defence for many people in public life when they come in for criticism or a bit of slagging.

All of this is not to say that begrudgery doesn't exist, just that the extent of it might not be as widespread as we assume. More poisonous to our self-esteem is the deeply embedded idea that we are a begrudging *nation* – that the idea of success in another person is almost unendurable to us. And that isn't true.

Take sport, for instance. The likes of Henry Shefflin or Brian O'Driscoll don't come in for begrudgery because the reason for their success is transparent. All you need to do is look at their performance on the pitch to know that they deserve to be there, and this applies even to divisive figures like Roy Keane. You might have been appalled by what he did in Saipan, but no one could argue that he wasn't a great player.

The begrudgery tends to kick in in other areas, where there is that suspicion that the person doesn't quite deserve all the success that they have attained – that they got it through knowing the right people, or family contacts, or dishonesty. There's always that suspicion that it's down to cute hoorism.

We normally associate cute hoorism with politics, but it pops up in other areas of life too. In 2013, the *Irish Independent* published transcripts of taped conversations between executives at Anglo-Irish Bank during which they discussed their strategy to save it. That consisted largely of 'You pull them in, you get them to write a big cheque and … they have to support their money.' In their dealings with the Financial Regulator, they used figures that they had 'pulled out of their arse' and seemed quite aware that what they were doing was unethical and might have profound ramifications for the country. But they didn't seem to care. Like an oily local politician, they thought only about the short term and their own advantage. They were posh boys with a private education, but this was cute hoorism at its most obscene.

The most striking thing about those tapes was that they showed these men to be free of any self-doubt. They may not have been sure if their strategy was going to work, but they were convinced that using made-up figures and specious arguments would not have any consequences for them. They were sure they would get away with it because of a culture in Ireland where dishonesty doesn't come with any consequences.

Bear with me, but the person to blame for all this may be Éamon de Valera. In 1987 the sociologist JP O'Carroll published an article entitled 'Strokes, Cute Hoors and Sneaking Regarders: The Influence of Local Culture on Irish Political Style'. His argument was that Dev created a template for how he wanted Ireland to be – one that featured maidens dancing at the crossroads, but also presented Ireland not so much as a country but as a large parish. *Everything* in Ireland was local. And this was not a fantasy picture. As we've mentioned already, the GAA in particular gave people a strong sense of connection to their county.

In parallel with this, Dev created a political machine that for decades was one of the most successful in western Europe, so much so that the idea of 'local' and 'Fianna Fáil' became enmeshed with each other (a machine that recognised the crucial importance of having its members embedded in the church and the GAA). The late journalist John Healy called it a 'moral community' where voting for Fianna Fáil meant voting for your area; not to do so was almost an act of betrayal.

The effect of this, according to O'Carroll, was that politics changed from being an expression of choice between competing ideas to one of pure expression: of declaring your loyalty, usually one that had been passed down to you from your family. That loyalty would be rewarded by the TD heading off to Dublin to get the goodies for you and your constituency, a process that might involve pulling a few strokes, but what of it? Sure, aren't they all at it?

We've talked about clientelism already. What's important here is the *aren't they all at it* attitude – where a bit of rule bending was seen as no harm if it got the job done. The *loyalty* was the important thing. And this wasn't just in politics. It filtered through all levels of society and still sloshes around today, eventually finding expression in two bankers discussing how they'd screw €7 billion out of this country. And if it *seems* to be everywhere, then of course we're going to suspect everyone of doing it. That guy is a millionaire? How did he do that? *Hmmm*, we think to ourselves.

It's also expressed in the marked reluctance of Irish politicians to resign once they have been caught doing something that they shouldn't. Not only are they reluctant, but many of them even seem shocked at the very suggestion – understandably so, as it doesn't happen that often.

Every time, we compare ourselves to the UK, where there is a tradition of falling on one's sword, old chap. But it's an apples and oranges comparison. Irish politics, as an expression of Irish society, is a *very* different place.

I could spend the rest of this book (and fill seven more) listing examples of cute hoorism, but I'll limit myself to just one. Not that this example is any more egregious than any of the others, just that under the torrent of scandals we've had over the last 20 years, it's been somewhat forgotten about.

In late 1989, the Fianna Fáil TD John Ellis was facing financial ruin. Stanlow Trading, the cattle-dealing, meat-processing business he'd established with his brothers, was going belly up. They owed over £500,000 to two banks, along with money to marts and around 80 farming families, many of whom had been paid with cheques that bounced. Now, most businesspeople in this situation would have to suck up bankruptcy, but if a TD is made bankrupt, they have to resign their seat. And no one wanted that. These were the days of the Fianna Fail–Progressive Democrat coalition. It had 84 seats – a one-seat majority. They didn't want John to go.

When the story was broken in 1999 by Charlie Bird in RTÉ, Ellis claimed that he had told his 'friend and colleague', the then Minister for Finance, Albert Reynolds, about his predicament. Reynolds, he said, had interceded with one of the banks on his behalf. When first asked about it, Reynolds said he had 'no specific recollection' of having done so. Then the next day he said he hadn't because there was 'no record' of any such contact having been made. He had a meeting with John Ellis, and now Ellis agreed with him.

Yet it was the case that in 1989, in an act of extraordinary generosity, Ellis's main creditor, National Irish Bank, accepted a settlement of £20,000, despite the fact that it was owed £263,450. Ellis also managed to pay off the two marts; that was about £25,000. The money came from the Fianna Fáil party leader's bank account, courtesy of Charlie Haughey. The farmers got nothing, though there was a story that one of the farmers had tried to get paid through a kidnap attempt.

At the time of the revelations, 10 years later, Ellis was chairman of the Oireachtas Joint Committee on Agriculture, Food and the Marine (an Albert Reynolds appointment), for which he was paid an additional £10,000 a year. Almost immediately, some started making the unhelpful suggestion that a man who had almost bankrupted a number of farmers might not be the perfect choice to run the Agriculture Committee.

Ellis resigned from the post, but it took him almost a month to go. Clearly, he'd learned some lessons from history. This was also an FF–PD coalition with a tiny majority, so reports appeared in some papers of Ellis 'telling friends' that if he was pushed off the Agriculture Committee he might quit the Dáil altogether, thus promoting a by-election – and if Fianna Fáil didn't win it, a general election. Nobody wanted that.

Ellis met with the then Taoiseach, Bertie Ahern. Ellis resigned from the committee but not the Dáil and Bertie paid tribute to his excellent work as a deputy, adding, several times, that Ellis had 'done nothing wrong'. At the time, TV3 dispatched a reporter to his Sligo–Leitrim constituency to see what people there thought about all this. The reporter could find only one person with anything negative to say about him. Everyone else said he was great and that they would vote for him again. That proved to be the case. He was returned to the Dáil in 2002, not long after he announced that he'd partially repaid some of the farmers via the IFA. However, he lost his seat in 2007 after his constituency was changed to Roscommon–South Leitrim. It probably didn't help that many of the farmers he had owed money to were based in Roscommon.

But that didn't end his political career. A few months later, Bertie Ahern appointed him to the Seanad. He's been out of the Oireachtas since the 2011 Fianna Fáil meltdown, but there are media reports that he's interested in running for the Dáil come the next election.

How does that make you feel? In the vast library of Irish political scandals, this is a relatively mild example, but the Taoiseach, Ellis himself and the voters who elected him apparently didn't feel anything untoward had happened here. It might make you feel that we can never get anything right in this country. But that's not just politics; there is a strain of fatalism in us. The actor-turned-travel writer Andrew McCarthy says, 'No one, I mean no one, does misery like the Irish.' We are possibly the only nation on earth to use our nationality as a negative adjective. If something goes wrong in this country, be it national, local or individual, we say, *That's just so Irish.* We spend €51 million on e-voting machines that we use only once because no one really likes them and because it might be possible to hack them. We then go on to spend €3 million to keep them in storage. That's so *Irish.*

This attitude may well have informed how many Irish people behaved during the days of the boom. Not everyone partied, but many did, and perhaps there was a sense that this is Ireland – it's bound to be a disaster eventually, so we might as well have a good time while we can.

Depressingly, that turned out to be true.

In fairness to us, as a nation we have experienced a lot of misery. Not even the 800 years of slavery stuff – we'll get to that – but what we've done in this century and the last, what we've done to ourselves. With gruelling regularity, up pops another revelation about how we have treated the most vulnerable, how we have been complicit in ignoring it: the child abuse scandals, the Magdalene laundries, the use of psychiatric hospitals as dumping grounds for unwanted relatives, the anti-sex, book-burning decades of Catholic rule.

It seems that with each new thump to our self-image comes a greater ability to embrace the idea of ourselves as failures. When the bodies of 796 babies were found in the old Bon Secours Sisters home in Tuam, Taoiseach Enda Kenny grimly warned that if an explanation was not found, 'Ireland's soul in many ways will, like the babies of many of these mothers, lie in an unmarked grave.' That revelation came in 2012, after the economic crash and myriad business and political scandals. In newspaper columns, the term 'failed state' was used regularly.

But it's nothing new. Flann O'Brien's novel *An Béal Bocht* (published in 1941) is a satire on Irish fatalism and a parody of the so-called Gaeltacht autobiographies, in which a person recounts the misfortunes of their lives and uses doleful phrases like *mar ná beidh ár leithéidí arís ann* ('for our likes will not be seen again'). The most famous example of this is the book *Peig*, first published in 1936, and used for decades after to torture and depress secondary-school pupils. But there are many other examples of the genre. The Irish did indeed invent the misery memoir.

Catholic guilt can't have been a help. Hundreds of years of being told that pretty much anything fun is a sin seems deeply unhealthy. But loath as I am to let the church off the hook here, Catholicism might not be the culprit. Our fatalism might be informed not by Catholic guilt, but *just* guilt.

Studies have been done on whether Catholics feel more guilt than people of other faiths, and most found little or no evidence for it. Instead, Catholic guilt seems to be more of a literary idea promulgated by English and American writers and reflected back to us. A study conducted in Britain in 2013 found that Muslims, Jews and evangelical Protestants feel *more* guilt than Catholics. Yet as we talked about previously, when we Irish present that golden version of ourselves to foreigners and each other, one word we never want to use is *No*. Irish people always want to be helpful and accommodating, even when we can't be. We say we'll turn up at a certain time when there's no chance we'll make it. We say we'll help someone move house even though we'll be in another country that day. We feel guilty about saying no, but then feel guilty about saying yes and not managing the thing we promised. This is *Irish* guilt.

But the main reason has to be our history – all those invasions, all those failed revolutions, all that hunger. Far more than any other event in our history, there is a body of opinion that believes the Famine has left a profound psychic scar within us. The Irish-American psychologist Garrett O'Connor (who is married to the actress Fionnula Flanagan) has claimed that the Irish suffer from a 'malignant shame' that developed because the Irish mind was 'enveloped and to a certain extent suffocated in an English mental embrace'. During hundreds of years of English rule, we learned to be furtive in our dealings with them and each other, and after the Famine we continued doing this. We acted like nothing happened.

Now you may be thinking this is a little spoofy. It's poetic-sounding speculation without offering much in the way of evidence. Yet consider this: Ireland was at one time one of the most densely populated places in Europe. But 170 years later it's still quite empty compared to most other developed countries. That's because *a million people* starved to death. This is a holocaust-scale event.

Given how much we talk about our history, how we still live with its reverberations, the Famine gets relatively little attention. This is strange.

The newspaper columnist John Waters, whose great-granduncle died during the Famine, thinks we are deliberately suppressing our feelings: 'There is a pain in Irish society that is not being admitted. It is there in the shapes of our society, in our congenital inability to realise our potential.' Here we have the language of psychotherapy, which is odd coming from Waters, given that in 2014 he declared depression to be 'an invention'.

His assertions were supported by some and greeted with much eye rolling by others, especially those more keen on embracing the 'global future', where there is an outright ban on negativity of any sort. Nonetheless, basic common sense tells us that he must be correct to the degree that the Famine would have had a profoundly traumatic effect on people at the time. The question is whether that trauma is still with us today. Fintan O'Toole has written about a kind of 'collective psychosis' similar to dissociation in psychiatry, where the mind can distance itself from experiences it does not wish to process. He argues that we somehow developed the ability to know things and not know things at the same time, an ability that allowed us to block out not just traumas such as the Famine, but all sorts of other horrors too, such as the abuse of kids in church-run industrial schools. It has also enabled double-think and breathtaking levels of hypocrisy.

In 2013 the historian Oonagh Walsh came up with an interesting theory: that the severe nutritional deprivation of the Famine period would have caused epigenetic change. Epigenetic change doesn't change the gene itself but it does change how it operates. It can, among other things, cause diseases such as cancer. It occurs naturally, but can also be caused by environment, lifestyle or diet.

Walsh's theory – and her research is still ongoing – is that this epigenetic change triggered higher rates of a number of diseases, including mental illness. This is backed up by some of the figures. According to the 1841 census, there were 1,600 patients in district asylums – out of a population of around eight million. By 1900, the population of the island had halved but there were 17,000 people in asylums and 8,000 'lunatics at large'. Of course, not all the patients were mentally ill. As we've mentioned, asylums have been used in Ireland as dumping grounds for unwanted people. Yet even this doesn't explain the enormous rise in figures. *Something* happened to our mental health in the years after the Famine. As to whether this has affected the way our society is shaped is probably unprovable either way. But it is clear that we can be down on ourselves – sometimes with justification, sometimes not. In our rush to self-criticise, we often forget just how far our country has come. In 2004, the Economist Intelligence Unit (EIU) devised a quality of life index based on a range of indicators, and Ireland came out on top.

The EIU measures others things too, such as democracy around the world and how it works in each country, and Ireland came 12th out of 167 countries. There are problems, of course, and we've already touched on a few of them. But we do live in a country where we can discuss them openly and we can do something about it. In the rating for civil liberties, Ireland came in first place, along with the likes of Norway, Sweden and New Zealand.

But guess what? It's not as straightforward as that. We can be very down on ourselves, ignoring what we've achieved while at the same time making wildly inflated claims about our importance. Here's a phrase you may have heard before: *punch above our weight*. Politics, the arts, sports – there's scarcely any area of human endeavour in which we don't claim that we are doing far better than one would expect for a small country.

In many respects these claims are true. To use that ghastly phrase, Ireland is a remarkably successful international *brand*, given that we are a country of just over four million people. Saint Patrick's Day is celebrated all over the world, there are Irish pubs and *Riverdance* and U2. We have made an inordinately large contribution to the global culture we spoke about earlier.

But sometimes it's not true. For many years it was claimed that we punched above our weight in Europe, based largely on our ability to extract huge grants out of Brussels. But given that the aim of these grants was to help Ireland catch up with the rest of the EU, it was probably based more on our ability to put on *an béal bocht*. We used our fatalism as a negotiating tool.

Our actual position in Europe was revealed during the bailout programme when the European Central Bank apparently made it plain that Ireland couldn't burn any bondholders, no matter what the eventual cost to the Irish taxpayer. Then in 2011, details of the forthcoming Irish budget were found to have been circulated among German politicians. But there have been signs of this kind of thing before. When we rejected the Nice Treaty in 2001, we had to vote on it again the following year to deliver the result Europe wanted, and the same happened when we rejected the Lisbon Treaty in 2008. And this was despite the fact that Irish politicians had explicitly stated that if Ireland voted No, the treaty would be dead. This made us feel important. Then when we did vote No, they told us we weren't important and we'd better vote Yes. We obeyed. It was reported at the time that President Sarkozy of France had flatly said, 'The Irish will have to vote again.' Just to remind you, the Lisbon Treaty came about only when French voters rejected the proposed EU 'constitution' in 2005. No one suggested they vote again.

It's a love–hate thing with Europe now. As the novelist Iris Murdoch observed, 'I think being a woman is like being Irish. Everyone says you're important and nice, but you take second place all the time.'

We were voting about Europe, but for some even this was, in reality, a vote about Ireland. The novelist Colm Tóibín voted in favour, 'not because I wanted to follow the Irish political establishment but because I despise it and need protection from it'. No matter what the issue, it's always about Us.

Our attitude towards Europe has changed as we've become more aware of the realpolitik of our relationship, which is probably no bad thing, and it doesn't seem to have profoundly affected national morale. But our relationship with other parts of the planet can be both contradictory and touchy.

There is the old saw of football support. Thousands of Irish people support Premiership clubs in Britain. They watch it on television and routinely wear English football club jerseys. In 2006, when the unionist Love Ulster organisation decided to stage a march in Dublin, they were attacked by so-called Republicans, some of whom were observed to be wearing Manchester United and Liverpool tops.

But even the most peace-loving Irish soccer fan would find the idea of cheering for the English football team repellent, no matter what the context. Nor would we cheer for them in rugby or athletics. During the 2012 Olympics in London, the RTÉ sport commentator Des Cahill tweeted, 'The English public are giving massive support to all the Irish athletes at the Olympics. It's embarrassing, knowing it is not done in reverse.'

The apparent inconsistency in football support has been explained by those who know more about soccer than I do (which is most people) as simply the capricious nature of the football fan. They will adore a player who plays for their chosen club, and then choose to hate him when he moves to another.

Another possible explanation is English arrogance. No matter what the competition is, they think they are going to win it. Which has a degree of truth to it, but not nearly as much as it used to. But none of this explains why we refuse to support the English when clearly they are so well disposed towards us. It leaves us with only history as an explanation:

we're still touchy. President Michael D. Higgins surely had this in mind when in 2014 he declared that he would be supporting England in the World Cup. Then again, he was on a state visit to England at the time. In the same year, an Irish publican in London banned his customers from cheering against England.

It's also arguable that the English support for Ireland doesn't soften our touchiness but makes it worse, because with that support comes the suspicion that a proportion of these English supporters *don't know* that Ireland isn't a part of the United Kingdom.

We've all met such people – in Britain and elsewhere – and it seems to really infuriate us. Even in Ireland, people can be enraged by the slightest suggestion that the Republic of Ireland isn't an independent country – just in case there are people living here who haven't heard the news.

In 2006, there was a complaint made to the Department of Education over an atlas produced by the educational publisher Folens. In it, Britain and Ireland were referred to as the *British Isles*. Some, such as the British Ordnance Survey, claim that it is a purely geographical term referring to the archipelago perched on the north-western edge of Europe that consists of Britain, Ireland and about 5,000 other islands. Others argue that this is disingenuous – that nothing can be completely devoid of history or politics. In 2005, the Sinn Féin TD Caoimhghín Ó Caoláin even asked a parliamentary question about the term. The answer, from the then Minister for Foreign Affairs, Dermot Ahern, was, 'The British Isles is not an officially recognised term in any legal or inter-governmental sense. It is without any official status. The Government, including the Department of Foreign Affairs, does not use this term.'

In the Good Friday Agreement, the term is avoided altogether and replaced with 'these islands'. The Irish Ordnance Survey uses the term 'the British Isles and Ireland'.

The row about the term pivots invariably around its provenance. It was recorded in the Oxford English Dictionary in 1577, though references to the archipelago go back as far as ancient Greek and Roman writers. Ptolemy referred to the larger island as *Great Britain* and to Ireland as *Little Britain*. But it's the *Britain* bit that's interesting. Most historians agree that *Britain* is derived from *Pretani*, which is how the inhabitants of both Great and Little Britain described themselves. It's an old Gaelic word.

But our sensitivity extends to far more than the Brits. We seem to have an expectation that foreigners should know a lot about our country – far more than we know about them. Or at least that's my experience. On my radio show it would not be unusual to interview half a dozen American authors in the course of a week, and a high proportion of them do one, or both, of two things:

1. Attempt to ingratiate themselves by making a reference to Guinness.
2. Attempt to ingratiate themselves by constantly referring to 'you guys in the UK'.

Sometimes these are professors at Harvard or Princeton, and sometimes they even have Irish names. Invariably it prompts an all-Americans-are-stupid reaction from some of the listeners, along with questions as to why I didn't correct them. I don't correct them because it would set an awkward tone for the rest of the interview. Certainly they are inviting such correction by volunteering their 'knowledge' of the UK and Ireland, but leaving this over-confidence (or arrogance) aside, why *should* they know much about Ireland? Would we expect them to know much about Belgium or Bulgaria?

Yet not only do we expect some degree of knowledge from foreigners, we also expect them to acknowledge our exceptionalism. For a country that can be overly self-critical, Ireland is very touchy when it comes to criticism from outside. Whenever a new edition of an international tourist guidebook is published, the comments about Ireland are invariably featured in the Irish media, particularly anything negative. And woe betide any public figure on the planet who might choose to make light-hearted comments about Ireland involving shamrocks, potatoes, our accent or alcohol. The Stereotype Police will hunt you down.

In 2015, the Australian prime minister, Tony Abbott, recorded a video message to mark Saint Patrick's Day. He waved his green tie at the camera, suggested that the main Irish contribution to Australia was singing and finished by saying, 'I'm sorry I can't be there to share a Guinness or two, or maybe even three, but like you I do rejoice in St Patrick's Day.' There was the usual blizzard of criticism, including a stern rejection of this 'stage Irish' portrayal from Enda Kenny.

Tony Abbott has said many stupid things in the past on a range of issues, so for him, this was nothing new. The video was cringe-worthy and full of stereotypes. But it would be, at the very least, disingenuous to suggest that Ireland doesn't trade on these stereotypes when they suit us. Enda Kenny might not like the suggestion that Irish people will drink on Paddy's Day, but when Barack Obama visits, where does he bring him? The pub. Every US president who has visited Ireland, along with many other international dignitaries, have had their photograph taken holding aloft a pint of Guinness while standing at a bar. These pictures have been beamed all over the world for many years and as such make up a visual shorthand to describe Ireland.

In marketing Ireland as a tourist destination, it's part of how *we* have described ourselves to the world. No wonder so many people think we're pissed all the time (that is, apart from the fact that many of us *are* pissed all the time).

As Terry Eagleton says, 'The Irish are endlessly fascinated by themselves.' We often assume that this fascination extends past our borders and into the minds of foreigners keen to get past the stereotypes. Not only that – these foreigners should think we're great. As we talked about already, that is often the case. People think we are charming and funny. We're a happy people.

Or we're not. It depends on what survey you look at.

Yes, I know. The contradictions are starting to grate now. Nonetheless, an international poll carried out in 2012 found the Irish to be one of the happiest nations on earth, scoring tenth overall. In response to the question 'how happy were you yesterday', we came out on top, with most people reporting nine out of 10. Yet in the same year, we were found to be one of the unhappiest nations. Across 58 nations, on average, 53 per cent of people reported being happy. In Ireland, however, only 45 per cent of us could manage it. According to the poll, Afghanistan was happier.

Such polls are hardly the stuff of rigid science and it's difficult to imagine an Irish person ever admitting to a stranger that they are unhappy; they wouldn't give them the satisfaction. But perhaps the two polls together give an accurate picture. Much like our ability to know something and not know something at the same time, we can be happy and not happy simultaneously.

However, a study in 2009 claimed that the Irish are the second biggest moaners in Europe, just behind the British. It calculated that the average Irish person grumbles for nine hours and 28 minutes a week, with the most complained-about subject being the weather. It's a curious thing about Irish people that when the weather is bad, which is often, we are *surprised*, as if we operate on the assumption that we have a Mediterranean climate.

On a more positive note, the Irish are, as Terry Eagleton put it, 'superlative mockers'. Except we don't describe it that way. Slagging is far more than just piss taking. When done properly it's close to an art form, where people inventively insult each other in a funny way. Good slagging is all about pitch and tone, and it's so funny that the slaggee can't really take offense when it's done properly. For the tone-deaf, a slag simply sounds like an insult, and as often as not it's embarrassing for the person who attempted the slag rather than the person who just got insulted.

Theoretically, in slagging, nothing is off limits, though in modern Ireland it has to be done carefully. Race, disability or sexuality could be potentially explosive areas, especially race. Slagging, or the way we do it, seems to be specific to Ireland, and the Irish ear is attuned to it. In 2008, a pipe fitter from the UK was awarded €20,000 because his Irish colleagues kept singing rebel songs and calling him a Brit.

Perhaps they were simply being cruel. Or perhaps it was the opposite, because slagging, apart from being a form of mutual entertainment, also fulfils a number of social functions. It keeps everyone in their place – or at the same level. It's difficult to think you're great when your friends will slag you about it. It's also a method of airing grievances. Couples in particular will slag each other in front of friends about issues they may be too nervous to raise when they are alone. In front of other people, the exchange is kept within safe parameters – because this is meant to be fun and no one wants to be made to feel uncomfortable by letting things escalate into seriousness.

But perhaps most importantly, slagging is an expression of fondness. We have great difficulty explicitly telling people we're proud of them, that we like them or even that we love them. So instead we insult them, albeit in a funny way. Only in Ireland is it the case that you can become socially anxious if your friends *aren't* insulting you; it could mean they don't care.

The ability to take a slagging is rated highly in our society because it means you don't think you're great. But there are many other ways in which we demonstrate – or feel we must demonstrate – our humility. In 2015 the supermarket chain Aldi ran a series of television adverts with the slogan *as Irish as* … The three aspects of Irishness it featured were our reluctance to be the first to hang up in a telephone conversation, our reluctance to make a fuss no matter how bad the circumstances and our inability to take a compliment.

The first we've dealt with already; it's part of that general disinclination to say goodbye at all. The second, the unwillingness to make a fuss, again goes back to not wishing to appear better than anyone else. It's a cliché of Irish life, yet it still does seem to be the case that we are reluctant to complain in public, especially in restaurants. As a result, many restaurants aren't that good at handling complaints. A waiter or waitress will perfunctorily ask *Is everything* OK? but usually won't hang around long enough to hear the reply. It's a part of our young food culture that we have yet to develop, but it also seems to be a function of the Irish way of thinking. As we've mentioned already, for a people keen to appear humble and self-critical, we don't take criticism that well. Often we don't complain because we assume that our criticism will be met with hostility.

In 2004, I presented a short series on RTÉ television called *Ireland Undercover*. It was a variation on the *Candid Camera* format, where we would use actors, hidden cameras and a psychologist to analyse how people were reacting to situations we had set up. In one, we created the World's Worst Waitress in a midlands restaurant. She left the diners waiting an inordinately long time and would then approach them carrying the menus, only to veer off at the last moment to have a long and loud conversation on her mobile phone. She got every order wrong. She was over-familiar with the diners, sometimes sitting at the table with them. She swore.

No one complained.

Several of them discussed complaining but didn't get as far as that. Some just exchanged looks. Some pretended to be amused. A mother and daughter disagreed on what to do. The daughter wanted to complain, but the mother was steadfastly against it. At first she wouldn't explain why, but eventually offered, 'If we complain, they'll spit in the food.'

As for our inability to take a compliment, that's more difficult to prove. But there is an urban myth – which later became an internet meme – that a Polish woman who came to live in Ireland thought that the word *Penneys* meant *thanks*. Every time she would compliment an Irish woman on her dress or handbag, the Irish woman would dismissively wave a hand and say, *This? Penneys.*

The fact that these Irish traits were presented as part of an advertising campaign represents an odd sort of postmodern meta-slagging. The adverts are slagging Irish people, and by slagging, we of course mean expressing affection for. It's presenting a number of Irish hang-ups, but through the use of humour and affection, thus making them okay. It has the effect of making us feel good about how bad we feel about ourselves.

While selling supermarket meat.

Modern Ireland is changing. We have got better at complaining and taking compliments. Because of globalised, but particularly American, culture, we are far more touchy-feely about our emotions. But there are still enough of us who are so emotionally stunted that we need insults to express how we feel.

It's weird and dysfunctional, yes, but it has also been a tremendous source of creativity. The work of the stand-up comedian Tommy Tiernan comes straight out of slagging culture. Much of what he says *is* slagging and thus, in that Irish reverse-logic way, is full of affection. Tiernan has also embraced the idea that nothing should be beyond slagging – because if you're not being slagged, you're being excluded. So, controversially, he's done material about Travellers and people with Down's syndrome. There have been complaints, of course, but Tiernan hasn't backed down and it doesn't seem to have negatively affected his career. Enough people seem to understand what he's doing and *why* he's doing it. It's difficult to imagine this happening in any other country.

Another trait of Tiernan's is that while he's very funny, there's also a strain of sadness to him, a melancholy, as if we all know that life is not going to end well, so we might as well laugh while we can. It is humour that keeps the dark at bay, if only for a little while.

It's not unique to him. The American politician and sociologist Daniel Patrick Moynihan has written that 'to be Irish is to know that in the end the world will break your heart'. Sadness and loss run like a six-lane highway through pretty much every aspect of Irish culture, and this is informed by our history, particularly that of emigration. Indeed, it can often seem like in Ireland there is nothing *but* history. 'History is a nightmare from which I am trying to awake,' says Stephen Dedalus in *Ulysses*. The likes of Joyce and Beckett tried to escape this through emigration, but that in turn became part of the sad emigrant's tale; it fetishised exile. Yeats tried to create the image of a Mother Ireland who would heal us from the past, but that only seemed to remind us of all that had been lost. It seems to be a repeating pattern in Irish artistic expression. The more we try not to mention the past, the more present it is.

This can be found in all sorts of culture, both high brow and popular. The songs of Thomas Moore, known as *Moore's Irish Melodies*, were essentially the pop songs of the 1800s, hits in both Britain and Ireland. Yet even though he was accepted by British society – his songs interpreted there as somewhat mawkish tales of old Ireland – many of them were interpreted here as sly references to the loss of our Gaelic past or the death of Robert Emmet.

Most pop music produced in Ireland today sounds largely the same as pop music anywhere else. It is essentially an international cultural product, which may explain the vehemently mixed reactions to *Riverdance*. As we've said before, it's an Irish contribution to global culture, which makes it not entirely Irish. It may *sound* Irish, but it's not sad.

Now this is not to say that your average Irish person spends a lot of time ruminating about Cromwell or the Black and Tans. It's just that hundreds of years of song and poetry and prose that couldn't help but mention the sadness have burned themselves into the culture and into how we view the world.

This is made more acute by the fact that up until 150 years ago, we described this sadness in Irish. In his book *Ireland and Irish America: Culture, Class, and Transatlantic Migration*, the historian Kerby A. Miller makes some interesting points.

Language is used to describe the world around us but also how we experience it. It cuts up and classifies those experiences through adjectives and nouns. But different languages do this in different ways. English, for instance, is a nominative language, which essentially means that 'I' is used to describe different sorts of experiences. I can say *I am writing* – this is an action that I choose to do; I have control over it. I would also say *I have blue eyes*, but this is not something I made happen or had any control over.

The Irish language is a stative-active tongue, meaning it makes the distinction between these two sorts of experience. As a result, it can be more specific. It can say *I am sad* in two different ways: *tá brón orm*, which means *sadness exists on me*, and *táim go brónach*, meaning *I exist sadly*. The first is stative, the second active. In the first, the sadness has been foisted on the person from outside forces; in the second, it is within them.

Apart from being hauntingly beautiful phrases (which must also be part of the allure), it also gives a stinging sense of what is happening, of the intense victimhood of starvation, of having to leave everything behind. Based on songs and letters home, Miller says that the Irish were the most homesick of all the emigrants to the United States – because it wasn't voluntary. Emigration *was put upon them*. They were exiles.

The inescapability of all this sadness is due, in part, to the fact that we like it. No one has ever done a count, so I'm going to stick my neck out and say that the vast majority of traditional Irish songs are sad and have endured, clearly, because people like them. In 2012, a study was carried out to discover why people listen to sad music. Appropriately, it was carried out by the University of Limerick.

Unsurprisingly, one of the reasons was a desire for connection – a need to find a song that matched a current mood. People also used music to trigger specific memories, to re-experience sadness as a form of therapy. These were the conscious reasons. But the researchers also identified a cognitive function whereby sad music provides a group bond. It puts sadness in the wider, human context – we're all sad together. Tonight, in some pub in Ireland, someone is singing a ballad that recounts some awful tale of death and loss and exile. And everyone is singing along.

The sadness also finds its way into our ordinary speech, usually in the most humdrum of circumstances. Irish people might be cautious about mentioning the latest political scandal in the newspaper, but they will always volunteer what they've read about a murder or a car crash, often in the same tone of voice they'll use to talk about their holidays or how the kids are doing in school. Irish parents will relay the news from home to their grown-up children, which usually consists of a list of who has passed away recently. Annette Freeman, who works on my show, is from Mayo. Her father has been known to say to her, 'You don't know him, but you'll never guess who died.'

This, arguably, is the more healthy side of our inherent sadness: we are not shy to speak about death or tragedy or physical illness. Mental illness is a different matter. If your daughter has cancer, your neighbours will cross the street to ask how she is and if there is anything they can do. If she's had a nervous breakdown, they'll cross the street to avoid having to ask. Or you won't have told them in the first place.

A warning on figures here. When it comes to mental disorders, statistics are calculated in different ways in different countries and the definitions of what constitutes a disorder also vary, making it tricky to compare Ireland to other countries. The mental health charity Aware estimates that 10 per cent of the Irish population is suffering from depression at any one time and that one in nine will suffer an anxiety disorder over the course of their lifetime. But these are estimates because only a fraction of these people receive the appropriate treatment.

The Mental Health Commission published a report in 2008 that looked at the economic cost of poor mental health in Ireland in 2006. The figure it came up with was €3 billion – about 2 per cent of GNP.

In 2015, the *Irish Examiner* published a detailed account of how many anxiety and depression drugs were prescribed in 2012. It was a total of 2.3 million prescriptions for 330,000 public patients. And that didn't include prescriptions under the Drug Payments Scheme or the Long Term Illness Scheme or private patients. The *Examiner* reckoned the figure is closer to half a million.

The study also showed that the level of prescription varied in different parts of the country. The lowest was Dublin South at 4.3 per cent of the population. The highest was Limerick at 10 per cent. Clearly, socio-economic status does play a part here: 47 per cent of the population of Limerick has a medical card as against only 20 per cent of Dublin South. Theoretically, these distressed people can be offered talking therapies such as counselling as an alternative to pills. But there's a waiting list. When the *Examiner* asked, the HSE said there were 478 people waiting longer than three months, 39 waiting longer than six months and six waiting longer than nine months. You'd take the pills instead.

How this compares to other countries isn't clear. The methods of measurement vary. Some studies say rates of depression in urban Ireland and the UK are the worst in Europe; others put it at about average. Around one-quarter of Europeans suffer from a 'mental disorder', but this takes in a range of conditions of varying severity, not just depression. Nonetheless, the fact that more than one-tenth of the Irish population feels the need to medicate is alarming, especially as this is a country where we don't like to talk about our feelings – where a lot of us wouldn't dream of going to a doctor. What are those people doing?

It becomes seriously worrying, though, when we look just at young people. A Royal College of Surgeons report released in 2013 found that one-third of young people are likely to have experienced some form of mental disorder by the *age of 13*. The rate increases to more than half by the time they reach 24.

There are international figures to compare with, and they are terrible. For 19–24-year-olds in Ireland, the rate of mental disorders is 55 per cent. In the US (which usually has the worst rates for depression and various mental illnesses), the rate is 52 per cent. It's 44 per cent in the UK and 39 per cent in Germany.

Of course, 'mental disorder' takes in a large basket of conditions, from feeling a bit down over a specific set of circumstances right up to psychotic episodes. At the milder end of the scale, you could argue that this is just the bumps of life rather than something that needs to be medicalised. Like most western countries, Ireland has seen a huge growth in the mental health 'industry' and an explosion in the number of counsellors and psychotherapists, in part because the area is still totally unregulated. Most are completely legitimate and the Irish Association for Counselling and Psychotherapy does practise regulation for its members, but in the morning, you could set up as a counsellor if you wanted to.

Having said all that, let's not underestimate the problem either. The College of Surgeons study found that one in 15 young people have engaged in deliberate self-harm and one in five have had suicidal thoughts.

Suicide is the leading cause of death for young people in Ireland. It is the fourth highest in the European Union, and it is notably high among young Irish men between the ages of 16 and 34. This is how common it has become: one study of

Irish men aged 18 to 34 found that *78 per cent* of them knew someone who had died by suicide.

Among the Irish as a whole, suicide rates doubled between 1987 and 1998, though this could just be that we became more comfortable recording deaths as suicides. Even now there is a proportion of deaths every year that are recorded as an accident or 'undetermined', and one can imagine how this could happen as a kindness to a grieving family.

Grimly, there is an international league table for suicide. Out of 100 countries, we are 47th. At least 500 Irish people a year take their own lives. The vast majority, 83 per cent, are male, and in half of all suicides, alcohol is involved.

Now of course this is not down to the Irish predilection for sadness. There are many factors: genetics, loneliness, grief, relationship breakdown, poverty, unemployment. The recession literally killed people. But our marked reluctance – especially among Irish men – to talk about anything but our feelings is certainly not a help. For such a sociable people, we can often be desperately alone.

Chapter 6

The Order of Melchizedek: Are We Open?

My mother's theology, if you could call it that, was expressed in one simple gesture. Whenever I might express any doubt or make a smart comment about the Roman Catholic project, she would extend a flat hand and point at it. In an ominous-sounding voice she would say, 'God has you in the palm of his hand.'

The ominous tone was deliberate. She didn't mean that I was in the palm of God's hand in the caring sense; rather, she was trying to communicate what a perilous position this was. God was more like a despot or a mafia Don. He owned us. Being in the palm of His hand meant that at any time He liked, He could use one of his divine thumbs to crush me out of existence.

For her, religious belief and adherence was more like a survival tactic. She never seemed to question what kind of a

God would act in such a petty manner. That in itself would be far too risky. God wasn't about rewarding us for being good. God – the Irish, Catholic God – wanted to punish us for being bad.

In this she was a product of the society she came from, in which it was taboo, even dangerous, to express dissent. Seán Ó Faoláin writes about the stern moralist priests who were common when he was growing up – the sort who would police dances or scour hedges at night, armed with a blackthorn stick that they would use to beat any courting couples. Priests were not teachers or guides or people serving their communities. Priests were there to be obeyed.

Ó Faoláin also writes that due to various historical factors, the church since the 1600s was 'a peasant church, much too poor and too harassed to develop an intellectual life either among its priests or its people. In the circumstances the church, not unnaturally, found it easier to rule by command rather than by advice or persuasion. It is still locked in that imperious tradition, unable or unwilling to admit that its flock has been developing ahead of it.'

We've seen how that imperious tradition played out when the catalogue of abuses emerged during the last 20 years. The church reacted the way it had always done – on the assumption that its authority was taken for granted. It's still struggling with the new reality. In 2010 I wrote a column for the *Irish Examiner* making the rather mild (I thought) point that while most Catholic children still make their confirmation and communion, the *meaning* of it seems to have changed, from being mostly religious to mostly secular. This prompted a letter from a Cork-based priest to tell me that I regularly engaged in 'anti-Catholic bashing' (ignore the double negative) and that the Roman Catholic Church would exist 'after the Moncrieff name is extinguished, as well as the townland in Perthshire where the name originates from'. One or two priests can, it seems, still rock the imperiousness.

Catholic control was about more than just the spiritual life of Irish people. It played out in a very real way in how Irish communities organised themselves. Together with the local GAA club, the Catholic Church has always been at the centre of things. It was where people went to meet each other, but also where they went *to be seen*. Regular attendance at church was a form of social capital, and the more pious-seeming it was, the better. To be regarded as a *good Catholic* was synonymous with being well regarded in the community, and the opposite was also the case. No wonder my mother was so fearful of pushing against this orthodoxy. In the Ireland she grew up in, it meant pushing against *everything*: against the community, the country, the universe. You couldn't possibly win.

As I wrote before, when we lived in London, 'Irish' and 'Catholic' were interchangeable terms. It set us apart from the heathen hoards that surrounded us. But this wasn't just a self-defensive posture because we happened to live in the land of the ancient oppressor. For my mother it was an expression of Irish exceptionalism. The Irish were not only Catholic, they were the *best* Catholics.

During our holidays in Ireland and even after we moved back, she would occasionally insist that we visit the Knock Shrine in Mayo. It was nearly always raining. We'd obediently walk in file behind kids in wheelchairs and middle-aged women wearing disposable translucent raincoats, droning prayers and going round and round and round the small church until we'd achieved a sort of punchy feeling, an odd dislocation that some may have taken to be a religious experience. At some point, usually if she thought that my attention was drifting, she'd insist on telling me *again* how the Virgin Mary appeared to a group of ordinary people (other saints and Jesus are reputed also to have appeared, but she never mentioned them) and how the sun danced in the sky, just as it did around the time of the Fatima apparitions in Portugal. This second detail seemed to be particularly important to her. And as I did on many occasions during her life, I had the distinct sense that she was trying to convince herself more than me – that if I were inclined to believe all this, it would make it easier for her too.

I wasn't inclined to believe. I was an annoying know-it-all teenager and so I would point out that the church did not require anyone to believe in this stuff. She'd tell me I was being immature and arrogant. She'd point to the huge number of people who went to Knock and to the repeated claims of miracle cures.

She always seemed personally offended by these exchanges. I think this was because by casting doubt on what happened at Knock, I was also casting doubt on the specialness of Ireland. Very few countries have had Marian apparitions. The British never did. Think of it: the Creator of the Universe, who almost never reveals himself on this earth, decides to appear in a poor, tiny village in the west of Ireland. How could this *not* be evidence of how singular Ireland is? All those centuries of oppression, particularly religious oppression, had a point because in the end the Irish were proven to be the favoured ones, just like the Jews. The Irish were right.

I have always been interested in religious belief. Some years ago I even wrote a book about it. What's fascinating is how over the centuries, religious beliefs have cross-pollinated. There is a striking similarity, for example, between some old Celtic gods and those of Vedic Hinduism from 5,000 years ago, the theory being that these beliefs travelled west and south from northern India and gradually adapted within each new society. Within India, Buddhism, Sikhism and Jainism were offshoots of Hinduism. In China, Buddhism and Hinduism mingled with traditional Chinese belief systems. In Japan, Buddhism influenced Shinto, which in turn gave us Tenrikyo. In Vietnam, Cao Dai absorbed bits of all of the above and Christianity.

Moving west, Vedic Hinduism influenced Zoroastrianism in Persia, which influenced Judaism, which begat Christianity. Christianity and Judaism gave us Islam and Rastafari. Islam also gave us the Bahá'í faith. Christianity mixed with a range of indigenous beliefs to produce hybrid religions practised by millions. In Europe, Christianity was gently grafted over the old Pagan beliefs, many of which were resurrected 2,000 years later in forms of Paganism. One could argue that there aren't many religions, just *one* religion with myriad adaptations.

By the same process, Irish Catholicism developed into something different from Catholicism in other countries. We've mentioned some of the reasons already, but another is the lack of a fully developed civil society in Ireland. In other European Catholic countries, there is a common acceptance of the primacy of the state; in some there is even the idea that the state stands for a set of shared values. In Ireland, especially during the 20th century, we never got around to doing that.

All we had was Catholicism, which tended to promote a moral code almost singularly concerned with our sex lives.

What's all this got to do with openness? Well, if the vast majority of people in a society adhere to one belief system (or are too nervous to buck against it), then that society is, by definition, not an open one. Catholicism, and the Catholic hierarchy, had a vast and pervasive effect on the laws we made, what we could and couldn't say, who we could have sex with, what we could read, what we could *think*. Up until the 1970s, the church had direct access to government ministers, who, all too often, would do the church's bidding. From 1929 until the late 1950s, the work of *10,000* authors was banned in Ireland.

Of course, given our propensity for rule bending, there were many individuals and sub-cultures in Ireland that dodged around these restrictions. The historian Diarmaid Ferriter says that 'during a century where there was an avowedly Catholic ethos, oppression and watchfulness, there was also no shortage of clandestine and illicit sexual behaviour.' And people read banned books. They talked. They thought. It is arguable that the Irish have always been an open people! We just had to appear not to be. Nonetheless, the Irish were subject to an attempt at nearly North Korean levels of mind control.

Thankfully, it didn't work, and for many reasons. The dramatic decline of the influence of the Catholic Church in Ireland is due to far more than the way it reacted to the sexual abuse scandals. That decline had been happening anyway, and for many decades, because the minds of Irish people had been opening up.

At the risk of again pointing out the obvious, let's make a distinction here between religious belief and religious adherence. One of the many clichés about the Irish is that we are a spiritual people (whatever *spiritual* means), and there seems to be some truth to that. That sad strain in Irish culture we talked about before naturally lends itself to an existential thoughtfulness, and the decline of Catholicism has not diminished this. If anything, it's given it a boost.

The point is that it's impossible to say if there's been a dramatic decline or not in the levels of belief in God, Jesus or whatever, just that fewer Irish people feel the need to express what beliefs they may have within the institutional Catholic Church. The *institution* has declined in influence. But God? That's up to you. The fact is that just a few decades ago, 95 per cent of Catholics regularly attended mass. The figure now is more like 35 per cent. As recently as 1985, when groups of people claimed to see a statue of the Virgin Mary move at a grotto in Ballinspittle, County Cork, the story was treated quite respectfully by the media. In 2009, when there were claims that the sun was dancing in the sky again at Knock and that the image of the Virgin Mary had appeared in a tree stump in Limerick, there was no attempt to contain the sniggers. In a 2007 survey commissioned by the conservative Catholic group the Iona Institute, only 5 per cent of 15–24-year-olds could quote the first commandment (to save you looking it up: you shall have no other Gods before me). About one-third didn't know where Jesus was born, while 35 per cent did not know what is being celebrated at Easter.

Combine all this with the popularity of anti-religious agitprop from writers such as Richard Dawkins, and it's arguable that the Dublin media, social media (Twitter is often vehemently anti-clerical) and some sections of the public have become so secular that it borders on intolerance. A 2011 study (again from the Iona Institute) found that almost one-quarter of Irish people would be happy if the Catholic Church disappeared from Ireland completely. Senator Rónán Mullen, a conservative Catholic, has complained that in secular liberal Ireland it's become almost embarrassing to admit that you are a person of faith. In 2012, when the boxer Katie Taylor returned from the Olympics with a gold medal and ascribed this to God, it was odd because no one in Irish public life says things like that any more. They used to all the time.

Everyone loves Katie Taylor. When it comes to the aforementioned Rónán Mullen and David Quinn of the Iona Institute, that's less the case. They've both been on my radio show many times and the reaction to them, particularly on Twitter, is invariably vitriolic. The anger isn't just towards the opinions they express (you'd expect that), but to the fact that they are *on the radio at all.* The generation that became somewhat politicised through social media, the death of Savita Halappanavar and the same-sex marriage referendum does at times display a disturbing intolerance when it comes to freedom of expression.

This cuts both ways. During the same-sex marriage referendum campaign of 2015, a proportion of the text reaction to Yes campaigners was nothing short of hateful, much of it sickly obsessed with what gay and lesbian people do with each other in the bedroom.

But freedom of expression is to a degree controlled by social mores. In 1950s Ireland, it would have been acceptable to publicly express the idea that Protestants and Catholics shouldn't marry. If such an opinion appeared in the media now there would be complaints, not just about the person expressing the idea but also the media outlet that gave them the room to do so. In 50 years' time, the same might be the case when it comes to same-sex marriage.

I digress. The rot started for the Catholic Church on New Year's Eve, 1961, when Raidió Teilifís Éireann launched. Prior to that, the country had spent a few decades culturally and economically cut off from the rest of Europe. But it wasn't sustainable, either economically or politically. To feed itself, Ireland needed to open up, and culturally, other influences were starting to creep in. BBC television had been available in the North for some time, while Ulster Television launched in 1958. Along the border counties and down the east coast, images from a completely different world were already arriving in the living rooms of Irish people. The Irish state felt compelled to act, partially out of a sense of demonstrating that it was as 'modern' as the North, and partially out of a perceived need to provide some sort of bulwark against Anglo-American culture. Not that everyone thought this a great idea. On the opening night, President Éamon de Valera admitted that he was 'somewhat afraid … [television] can be used for incalculable good, but it can also do irreparable harm'.

Many Irish people shared these concerns. It was somewhat odd for them, having these strange flickering pictures in their living rooms. There are many stories about people who wouldn't get undressed or discuss family issues when the TV was on. I can remember that the television in Killala had a blue piece of transparent plastic sellotaped to it, the explanation being that it made the black-and-white picture more 'colour' and that it was a protection against the rays from the screen, which might give you cancer.

Not that this seemed to stop anyone. In 1963, 237,000 Irish households had a television. A decade later the figure was 536,000 households, most of which had RTÉ only. By the end of the 1970s, 83 per cent of Irish homes had a telly.

But making television programmes is both costly and time consuming, so almost immediately Dev's hope that it would 'promote the national character' was under threat. In the first year, RTÉ managed only 275 hours of home-produced shows, with the rest of the schedule filled largely with UK and US imports. Every evening, Irish viewers were exposed to a more cosmopolitan, more liberal world, not to mention the glittering allure of consumerism.

Within a few years though, RTÉ was producing over 1,000 hours a year of programming, much of it drama. The first Head of Drama at RTÉ was Hilton Edwards, who along with his partner, Micheál Mac Liammóir, was one of the grand elders of the Gate Theatre. With that kind of background, he had little interest in the sort of social-realist TV drama being made in England. Most of the productions he oversaw were romantic and escapist and often heavily moral in tone, with the morality usually emanating from a priest or a nun. Many of the plays even dealt with specifically religious themes, such as ecumenism.

However, as the decade moved on, influences from across the water did start to seep in. RTÉ made its first serial drama, *Tolka Row*, in 1964 – an Irish version of *Coronation Street*. It introduced a largely rural country to life in a working-class Dublin suburb, an environment as alien to most Irish people as Singapore.

After *Tolka Row*, the series *The Riordans*, *Bracken* and *Glenroe* all depicted rural life. Each one addressed various issues, but in a generally gentle way (though the character of Biddy McDermott in *Glenroe* – the equal of any man in male-dominated agriculture – was a mildly radical idea). Not that these shows were completely free of controversy. The occasional episode, especially ones that might deal with marital breakdown or sex, usually came in for some degree of criticism.

RTÉ couldn't win. Conservatives accused it of pushing a foreign, liberal agenda, while liberals felt it was profoundly conservative – a push–pull that often engendered a neurotic anxiety within the organisation. Like any branch of the civil service, acutely aware of criticism from above and below, RTÉ has often been a place where it was not wise to explicitly state an opinion, or to express an opinion at all. The writer of *The Riordans*, Wesley Burrowes, put it this way: 'It will rarely happen that a specific person in authority will say "This is unacceptable". He will more likely say that, while he personally sees nothing wrong with it, his immediate superior is not so broad-minded and perhaps it might be better to change it. If you ever meet the superior, he will say the same about his superior, and so on up the ladder. My own view of the Tic (if I may use this as a collective term for nervous men) was that they tended to pre-judge the conscience of the viewers, instead of consulting their own.'

But the Tic didn't inoculate RTÉ from getting in trouble. By far the most controversial drama on RTÉ during the 1970s – perhaps the most controversial it has ever produced – was *The Spike*. It began a 10-week run in January 1978 but only got as far as episode five. Set in a technical school (the former name for VEC colleges) in a poor urban setting, it aimed to make bold observations about poverty, education and Ireland's burgeoning underclass. But all that was completely ignored when the far more controversial subject of boobs hoved into view. Episode five featured a life-drawing class with a nude model, and despite the fact that the model was shot in such a way that no nudity was on show (for much of the scene she was behind a screen), righteous outrage exploded around the country. The founder of the League of Decency (there was one back then) claimed to have had a heart attack brought on by all that naked Irish flesh. RTÉ pulled the series, a decision endorsed by the then Taoiseach, Jack Lynch, and by a majority of viewers, according to a survey conducted by RTÉ afterwards.

Yet those same viewers had far less difficulty with the foreign programmes RTÉ transmitted, such as the US mini-series *Rich Man, Poor Man*, which featured Olympian amounts of sex and was a huge hit (it also launched the career of Nick Nolte).

However, it would be unfair to categorise RTÉ as a monolithic organisation, afflicted with a uniform neurosis. It's more like the European Union: a series of nation states with an (ostensibly) common purpose who also jostle for position and power and resources and perhaps have other aims that they haven't told the others about. This can, of course, lead to even more neurosis, but also to creativity. The documentary series *Radharc* stemmed from an idea from that bastion of clerical power, John Charles McQuaid, that Catholic values could be transmitted via the cathode ray tube. But *Radharc* developed into a brave and innovative series that zeroed in on social justice issues around the world. Indeed, it's arguable that

Radharc, staffed with clerics, was able to operate outside the reach of a government that desperately wanted to control all of RTÉ's output. Certainly it took the news and current affairs division a long time to shake off the template of the obsequious interview with the government minister. Nonetheless, *Hall's Pictorial Weekly* – which morphed out of the inoffensive *Newsbeat* – consistently poked fun at successive governments and got away with it. The popularity of the show no doubt protected it, though there is a story – and I have no idea if it's true or not – that the production team would selectively destroy tapes, thus making it far more difficult to follow up on complaints.

But the programme that created the largest amount of disruption was *The Late Late Show*, not just about the content it covered but about the *way* it presented itself to the viewers. It was a live show, and through Gay Byrne's presentation style, it constantly reminded the viewers that this was the case. Byrne was also producer and opted to eschew US television slickness in favour of a more casual method, where the bones of production were constantly on show. He'd talk to the floor manager or ask questions of researchers who were off camera or issue instructions to the director: *you can roll it there, Colette* became part of the national lexicon. The 'liveness' added to the zing of the show – potentially, anything could happen – and also partially insulated it from criticism. If someone made a controversial statement, Byrne and his production team could legitimately claim that they hadn't known it was going to happen.

There was also an element of this in Byrne's interviewing style. He was rarely aggressive with his interviewees and managed the knack of seeming to be as surprised as anyone if the interview took a shocking turn – as if he hadn't intended to do this. If he was going to interview someone embroiled in some particular controversy, for instance, he would often not ask them about it. Then he would appear to be wrapping up the interview – usually by telling them how wonderful they were – and then, almost as an afterthought, slip in the killer question.

The 'casualness' of the show also felt very Irish in nature, which not only drew in the audience but also had an effect on the *way* Irish people watch television. This is my own theory, and I've no evidence to back this up. But certainly my experience is that in Ireland, when you'd visit someone on a Friday night, they'd leave the television on. This was not considered rude; it was almost as if Gay Byrne was also a visitor. People would talk about other matters but also keep glancing at the TV, and sometimes the conversation would turn to what was on the screen. This habit has continued in the modern era on Twitter.

But the real dynamite of *The Late Late Show* was the studio audience, who were encouraged to take part in the discussions. These were ordinary people, just like the people at home. For the first time, the country witnessed people like them confronting authority figures. It happened to John Charles McQuaid in the very first series, and it happened countless other times during the Byrne era. There was rarely a season without a controversy or a denunciation from the pulpit, an apology from RTÉ and people after mass asking each other, *Did you see The Late Late?*

The number of times various figures called for the show to be axed, or Byrne to be fired, must run into dozens at least, as do attempts at analysis of what Byrne was up to, of what kind of man he is. There's no doubt that he was aware of the global tides of change, of the sorts of things Irish people would be interested in hearing about. But that's not the same as saying that he had a liberalising mission. Certainly anyone I've met who has worked for him has said that he was open to any sort of item idea, but he would always ask the same question: *Can they talk?* For him, the show was the thing. As a TV producer, he didn't care about status or political office, because in the studio everyone would be judged by the same criteria: *Can they talk?* It was this egalitarian approach that had a profound effect on how the Irish came to judge public figures. No matter who they were, if they were pompous or hypocritical or tedious, the audience, with just some gentle nudging from Byrne, would find this out. Fintan O'Toole has written that 'being boring was the new mortal sin, and Gay Byrne was the one dispensing the penance'.

Gay Byrne isn't perfect, of course. Over the years he's had lapses of judgement and squads of critics accusing him of liberalism, conservatism, pomposity and cowardice, among many, many other things. But it would take some considerable meanness of mind not to accept that he was a brilliant television producer. Perhaps he didn't have a greater didactic purpose, but why should he have had? His attitude seems to have been that it was his job to produce television, not change society. Change may have come about as a result of ideas aired on *The Late Late Show*, but that change came from society, not Gay Byrne. Indeed, the ideas came from a number of television sources. *The Late Late* may have been the biggest thing on RTÉ, but there were any number of US and UK television shows also being screened that showed how life was different elsewhere. *Who shot JR?* was the start of globalisation.

At the same time, radio was also chipping away at the certainties of Irish life, albeit in a slightly different way. The 1970s and 1980s were still decades where the man went to work and the woman stayed at home and minded the kids. Daytime radio during those decades was predominantly for, and increasingly by, women. Once again, Gay Byrne was in the thick of it. *The Gay Byrne Hour* (later *The Gay Byrne Show*) launched in 1973 and quickly established a format that relied heavily on letters from listeners, virtually all of them women. The subjects ranged from the trivial to the serious and left little out: divorce, separation, sex, children, relationships. It wasn't so much about discussing issues as a forum where women could express their experiences – and get reactions from other women. With the men at work, it began to feel like a safe place where women could talk to each other.

In 1984, a 15-year-old schoolgirl named Ann Lovett died giving birth beside a Marian grotto in the town of Granard, County Longford. Her baby also died. Everyone in the town claimed they didn't know she was pregnant. It was yet another sickening example of silence and moralism trumping compassion. Some time afterwards, a poet named Christopher Daybell wrote to express his horror to the then Catholic Primate, Tomás Ó Fiaich.

It's not known exactly what Daybell wrote, but the reply he received, written on behalf of the cardinal, said: 'Why she chose to keep her secret will never be known … I think her sad death reflects more on her immaturity than on any lack of Christian charity amongst the family and people with whom she lived.'

This letter didn't emerge until decades later, but it reflects how the imperiousness we spoke about earlier was still in full force in the 1980s. There were few places where a woman could be heard, but *The Gay Byrne Hour* was one of them. Ann Lovett's death prompted a massive amount of mail into the show, much of it from women who had had similar experiences. They'd been unaware of how babies were made or they simply hadn't been careful. Some had been raped. Some had been raped by family members. Their pregnancies were a source of shame. The women were kept hidden or sent off. The babies were put up for adoption or raised by a relative. Or they were killed at birth.

There were so many letters that they decided to devote an entire show to them, read out in turn by Byrne and two actors. It was one of the most harrowing 50 minutes ever produced on Irish radio.

At the end of that decade, *Women Today*, hosted by Marian Finucane, took to the air. More issue based, it followed on from a documentary that Finucane had presented earlier in the year in which she'd accompanied a woman travelling to England to have an abortion. *Abortion: A Woman's Experience* was transmitted outside of primetime (primetime on radio is during the day) and so generated relatively little controversy, though it did win a Prix Italia award. *Women Today*, however, took to the air with an editorial policy that nothing should be taboo. The first show was on sex education.

Women Today was the subject of constant battles within RTÉ, with most of the objections being that these kinds of subjects shouldn't be broadcast during the day. There were attempts to move it to another time-slot. Yet the programme won a Jacob's Award and some years later transformed into *Liveline*.

Since the 1960s, our national discussions on the national broadcaster have been invariably negative. It's hidebound and conservative. It's full of raving lefties. It pays its presenters too much. It can't do comedy. It can't do chat shows. The news is biased, too soft or too hard. The license fee isn't worth it. I worked there for over a decade and all too often the experience was infuriating. There was paranoia, arrogance, cute hoorism – a system that seemed to punish creativity but reward sneakiness. Yet despite all that, its contribution to Irish life – to opening up our society – is incalculable. It might be no harm for us to be a bit less Irish and occasionally recognise that.

But just occasionally. We don't want them thinking they're great.

It's certainly arguable that during the 1970s and 1980s RTÉ Radio did as much, if not more, for the cause of feminism than any other movement or campaign. It alerted hundreds of thousands of Irish women to the reality that they were not alone in feeling like second-class citizens. And while Irish women began to find a voice on radio, the country as a whole found that they could view on television, and make judgements about, those in society who had previously been untouchable.

When put together, this started to have a devastating effect on the authority of the Catholic Church. Politicians, keenly aware of the need for public support to continue in office, quickly learned to adapt to the demands of TV in particular. Still convinced of its invincible authority, the church did not.

There were many battles left to fight, but the Catholic Church began to lose all of them. In 1985, the bizarre restrictions on the sale of contraceptives were lifted. In 1993, homosexual acts were decriminalised. Two years later, divorce was finally made legal in Ireland.

During the same-sex marriage referendum campaign of early 2015, I recall walking through the centre of Dublin and gasping at the sight of a Vote Yes poster with *Fianna Fáil* at the bottom of it. It seemed to crystallise how much, and how quickly, this country has changed. Unlike most other European countries, we didn't have an industrial revolution and the social change which that engendered. We didn't participate directly in the world wars. We didn't have a suffragette movement or a sexual revolution. We didn't swing that much in the Sixties. Most western countries eased into modernity over an extended period of time. In Ireland, all the change seemed to happen all at once, and it's astonishing how well we have coped with it.

Same-sex marriage was voted in by a massive majority – 62 per cent – which means not just that the Yes side won the political battle, but that they also *won the argument*. It couldn't be put down to a well-funded liberal 'elite' foisting their trendy ideas on everyone else. Everyone else had a gay son or daughter or cousin or neighbour and had come to realise that they had to be treated equally. Almost always, politics has an element of self-interest for the voter. This was one of the few times in the history of the state when the vast majority were being asked to vote so as to help others. And they did.

But 62 per cent in favour also means 38 per cent against. However, it's not clear what reasons these people had for voting against the proposition; they were probably various. No doubt there were some who felt the whole idea was disgusting and unnatural, and others who were swayed by some of the bogus arguments over surrogacy and the 'right' to a mother and a father. No doubt there were some who felt their religious belief prevented them from voting Yes, even if they wanted to. In the course of writing this book I was told the story of a very traditional Catholic mother who would not countenance voting anything but No. Yet when the result was announced, she expressed delight to her Yes-voting daughter. That's Irish Catholicism at work.

At least half the country grew up in the era when 'immoral' meant 'sexual'. Women were either whores or madonnas. Sex was dirty and something you should really only do to have children. You certainly wouldn't do it to someone you loved or respected. Generations of Irish people have grown up struggling with this perverted view of sexuality, so you'd think that we'd still be a little bit screwed up about it. The statistics, at least, would seem to indicate the opposite.

There is not that much research into the sex lives of Irish people. However, in 2005, the condom manufacturer Durex did commission a global sex survey across 41 countries, and the Irish came out of it looking reassuringly, well, normal.

The average age when Irish people first have sex is 17.3 years, which is about the same as the global average. In terms of partners, the Irish number is 11.1, above the global figure of nine. Around 12 per cent of us have had an extramarital affair, 62 per cent have had a one-night stand and 20 per cent have had a gay experience. Irish people have sex 97 times a year, just below the global average of 103 times. You're wondering, of course: the Greeks do it the most, at 138 times. The Japanese, God love them, only manage it 45 times a year. An *Irish Times* sex survey published in June 2015 produced largely similar results, though it also showed indications of willingness to experiment. It found that 16 per cent of people had had group sex, 21 per cent had engaged in BDSM and a majority – 58 per cent – had used sex toys.

However, while we may have ditched our hang-ups, there may still be a little work to do on improving our technique. According to a survey carried out by *Women's Health* magazine (which might not have as much scientific validity), seven out of 10 Irish women say they are not happy with their sex life.

Now there *may* be a reason for this. In 2012, a professor of psychology at the University of Ulster, Richard Lynn, published a study listing the average penis size of 113 nationalities. Disturbingly, the Irish were the second smallest in Europe. However, if you're an Irish man you'll be happy to hear that Lynn has been widely derided by many of his peers for what they claim is shaky science – not just in the area of mickey size, but also his contentions that white people are smarter than other races and that men are more intelligent than women.

So leaving aside the research of a barking eugenicist, the Irish are pretty much the same as every other western nation, which is a comfort, but something of a worry too. Like every other country with broadband connections, the access to pornography is all too easy, especially for young boys who may grow into manhood with a strangely skewed idea of what sexuality entails. It's too early to say if this worry will flower into something far darker, but it's certainly something we need to counter before that happens.

The decline of Catholic influence and the opening up of Ireland is about far more than just being okay with nookie.

It's also had a tremendous influence on the sorts of ideas we are now prepared to entertain. As we said earlier, even though many people may have turned away from mainstream Catholicism, it doesn't necessarily mean that they have stopped searching for a meaning to their lives. Inevitably, this has had mixed results, depending on your point of view. Atheism and Humanism have become mainstream, as have so-called New Age ideas. Both Dublin and Cork now host annual Mind Body Spirit Festivals where you can find Ascension teachings from the Alpha and Omega order of Melchizedek, get rebirthed, understand your past lives, learn about tai chi and reflexology and of course buy a book or DVD by Deepak Chopra.

Such ideas can easily be criticised for being faddish and blithe. It's spirituality-lite. There's not much work and certainly little thought involved. A lot of it is essentially meaningless. A lot of it is incorrectly cut and pasted from various religions and mixed up with other ingredients that are simply made up. A lot of it seems self-obsessional – it's all about You rather than Us. It doesn't describe your place in the universe so much as make *you* the universe.

But so what? As long as you aren't doing anyone any harm, fire ahead. In the same way that television has become a leveller among people, so too are we experiencing something of a levelling when it comes to belief. Looked at dispassionately, *any* belief that we can lump into the general area of 'spiritual', be it Islam or rebirthing, is as ridiculous – or not – as any other.

On my radio show we do occasionally interview people with some ideas that you could describe as on the fringe. I've talked to a number of people who have announced the date for the end of the world (they never return your calls after the date passes), at least two people who claimed to be the reborn Jesus, people who talk to aliens, people who've had sex with aliens, time travellers, Bigfoot hunters and one man who had a 'harem' of cars that he liked to make love to.

The vast majority of listeners enjoy this sort of thing as a bit of fun, but invariably there are two minority reactions: 1. People who have similar ideas, i.e. they too talk to aliens. 2. People criticising us for 'taking advantage' of a person who is 'clearly sick'.

This is of course anecdotal, but in my experience the reaction of the first type of listener has been steadily increasing. It may be the case that they were always there but afraid to speak out – or it's the result of exposure to the internet.

The second reaction is somewhat presumptuous, as it assumes that an unusual idea stems from mental illness or that people with a mental illness are incapable of coming to their own conclusions, however odd. We tend to choose people who have a website promoting their ideas (as often as not, those websites are also selling various products) or people who have written a book, the (admittedly) crude logic being that if they are trying to make a few bucks out of it, they can't be that ill.

Generally speaking, I've been pretty comfortable that we are not taking advantage of these people. In 2008, I interviewed a woman, Lorna Byrne, about her book *Angels in My Hair*, detailing how she's been seeing angels for most of her life and how these angels not only guide her, but also pass on messages on a vast range of subjects. The book has been translated into 30 languages. She's followed it up with several more, she has a website and she seems to spend a lot of her time travelling around the world giving inspirational talks (apparently 'self love is the best love'). She's certainly making a few bucks. Yet it was one of the few interviews where I did feel distinctly uncomfortable afterwards. To me, it sounded like what she was describing was schizophrenia.

Nonetheless, the interview got a massive reaction, with a huge proportion claiming that they too see angels or that what Lorna said made perfect sense to them. Part of the new openness does seem to entail accommodating a dizzying range of beliefs in Irish society, no matter how nonsensical they might seem to be to others.

The same applies to politics. Again, thanks to the internet, there's been a rise in the number of Irish people who subscribe to ideas that are generally grouped under the title of conspiracy theories. This isn't about aliens, but rather speculation on who is really running the world and this country. One of the main ideas is that a group of a dozen or so Jewish families (sometimes called the Illuminati) is edging the planet towards a One World Government. And if that's true, then potentially so is everything else: 9/11 was an inside job, commercial jets are regularly spraying us with mind-control agents, the US has a secret facility that can control the weather. On most days, there's a dribble of emails into the radio show upbraiding me for not knowing what's really going on.

Ireland's most famous exponent of a lot of these ideas is Jim Corr, who has been on the show to talk about them. He comes across as a perfectly agreeable fellow. His website, www.jimcorr.com, goes into lavish detail on many of these subjects, though as of June 2015, it was down for maintenance. This may or may not be connected to speculation that the Corrs are about to re-form. But that could just be a conspiracy theory.

Then again, conspiracy theories may not be altogether unreasonable, given what we know *does* happen. For instance, the Bilderberg Group, a favourite of conspiracists (or 'truthers'), is an annual meeting where the fabulously wealthy rub shoulders with the fabulously powerful – and it all happens in private. The underlying idea behind the meetings, which have been running since 1954, is that these people can say what they *really* think without it being reported in the media. That is somewhat unsettling. We are (or should be) painfully aware in this country of how businesspeople and politicians so easily convinced themselves – over some nice steaks and a bottle of Château Latour – that running a country as a private concern was for the good of everyone.

Those fancy dinners were a hallmark of the Celtic Tiger, as was the introduction of *food culture* into Ireland. Food culture came as part of a package under the general title of *lifestyle*, along with decking and nice lamps. These weren't just *things*, but products that carried with them an emotional weight – the promise of a Mediterranean-style happiness where it would always be sunny and we'd sit outside and we'd all have great friends, who would love us all the more for the way we slow cooked that lamb shank. It was pure marketing, and during the Celtic Tiger in particular, we embraced it lovingly. This enthusiasm was perhaps tinged with the idea that this was how other people had lived all along. Now it was our turn.

We rushed into it so enthusiastically that it quickly became a matter of middle-class mortification if you mispronounced quinoa or didn't know that Shiraz and Syrah come from the same grape. During the Celtic Tiger years, restaurant prices swelled to taking-the-piss levels – and not just in the high-end places. In 2003 in Cork Airport, I was charged €5.80 for a sandwich. It was chicken and stuffing. It was okay.

The media drove a lot of this, inventing the mythology of an Irish food tradition (which there isn't; even Irish stew was invented in England) while encouraging us to keep up with our Jamie Oliver-ised global neighbours. I have been part of this media push too. For the last decade I've presented a weekly wine-tasting slot on my radio show while also providing the voice-over for the TV show *The Restaurant*, where Irish celebrities run a commercial kitchen for a night. It was an indicator of just how important food has become to our self-image that celebrities and politicians felt there was something to be gained from showing off their culinary skills. Some were clearly coached beforehand; others were more political. When Enda Kenny appeared on the show in 2006 he wanted to use two types of black pudding in one dish because they were from opposite ends of his constituency.

But sometimes the ordinary diners who turned up were just as interesting. Most came for the adventure of a free dinner and seeing a TV show get made, but invariably there would be one or two – always men – who turned up to show off how much they knew about wine and food. Sometimes the self-importance was astounding. Living, breathing Celtic Puppies, though quite a few of them weren't puppies.

Wonder how they are doing now.

Food culture in Ireland was almost entirely imported, though that doesn't necessarily make it a bad thing. It did stimulate production of various products in the agri-food sector, such as cheeses, and in the years since the crash the restaurant industry seems to have become a bit more realistic, a bit more aware that they can't market themselves on the basis of snob appeal any more. It's about having a nice dinner, and in this respect we are the same as most other western nations. Food culture is a global phenomenon, and we're sitting at the table with everyone else.

Where we would like to still regard ourselves as distinctive, though, is in the area of creativity. Any tourist brochure will rattle through the names Joyce, Yeats, Beckett, Wilde, but these are all writers from the last century. Most of them emigrated, and one could argue that their art, at least in part, came from the repressive pressures of the society they were born into. In 21st-century Ireland, where we are all trying our very best not to be like that any more, have we brushed away the societal grit that can lead to the need for self-expression? If, in time, the Irish learn to say how they are feeling out loud, will this cancel the need to represent it in plays or books or films or music?

There's very little sign of this. Thanks largely to tax breaks and the Irish Film Board, the film industry has grown dramatically in the last 15 years or so and is now valued at around €550 million a year. A large number of high-budget TV shows and films have used Ireland as a base. More significant is the growth of home-based production. As the trade magazine *Variety* pointed out in 2010, at the turn of the century there were 'only two Irish filmmakers anyone had ever heard of' (Neil Jordan and Jim Sheridan), while 10 years later there were about a dozen. What's also impressive – and this includes Irish animated films – is how few of them have been duds; the standard has been very high. In global terms, the Irish film industry is tiny, but it is fair to say that in terms of reputation – here comes that phrase – Ireland does punch above its weight.

The same argument could be made for Irish theatre, though it has a longer tradition to draw upon. It's been tougher for theatre, though. Theoretically, an Irish movie can look all over the world for financial backing. Theatre productions are more constrained and have struggled as a result. In the late 1990s and into the start of this century, there was a flurry of new theatre companies being formed. But after the crash, many of them had their Arts Council funding cut or taken away altogether.

However, there have been signs of a recovery. Irish theatre attendances went up in 2014, and the Abbey Theatre, after cutting costs, went back into profit that year.

Of course, that could just be from tourists. The Abbey doesn't frisk people for passports on the way in, but the Arts Council does release annual figures for attendances at 'arts events', the vast majority of which were theatre performances. In 2014, 65 per cent of Irish people attended one such event, an increase of 9 per cent on the year before. It's also 9 per cent higher than the North and 13 per cent higher than Britain. We're not just showing off, then. We *do* like the artsy stuff.

It's in two areas, though, that Irish culture has been the most successful, both at home and abroad: writing and music. We've already mentioned the Big Four names who are towering figures in our cultural history. There was a time when 20th-century Irish writers would agonise about having to operate in the artistic shadow of James Joyce. You don't hear that so much any more, and this may be because Yeats, Beckett, Wilde but particularly Joyce have been appropriated by the tourism industry. *Ulysses* was a book so difficult to read that the zealously puritan Irish government didn't even bother to ban it, yet its image today is one of jaunty accessibility.

It's something to do with eating a nice breakfast, wearing a straw boater and strolling around Dublin. Indeed, the book *Ulysses* (which Roddy Doyle once suggested could do with a good edit) has become increasingly distanced from the festival Bloomsday, on which the action of the book is set. The celebrations for the 100th anniversary of Bloomsday in 2004 went on for five months, culminating in an event where 10,000 people crammed into O'Connell Street in Dublin to eat breakfast. You've got to wonder how many of those people had actually read the book.

The point is that a lot of this has virtually nothing to do with modern Irish writing. Irish writers of all varieties have got on with the job of producing work, and it's arguable that we are doing *better* now than the age we constantly hark back to. Yes, Ireland has produced some of the greatest writers of all time, but in terms of sheer quantity *and* quality, we are still doing that. This is not even remotely scientific, but I did it anyway. I went to the Wikipedia page that lists 'Irish writers'. The total number, which stretches back as far as the 7th century, is 311. I then deducted all the dead ones, and the remaining figure was 144. According to Wikipedia, around half of the Irish writers of note are still alive, and Irish literature is flourishing despite a steady decline in book sales over the last five years.

Part of the reason for this increase is globalisation. Genres that previously wouldn't have been that big in Ireland, such as popular fiction, crime novels, comedy and books for kids and young adults, are now being produced by Irish authors. The memoir, which at one time might have been regarded as a bit self-indulgent, has also become popular. On top of that we are still producing literary writers with substantial international reputations. Roddy Doyle, Anne Enright, Colm Tóibín, John Banville, Sebastian Barry and Joseph O'Connor are just some of the Irish writers who win prizes for their work all over the world. And a lot of the time, this isn't even reported in this country.

Why we've always produced great writers – why we continue to do so – is a subject area littered with clichés and academic tomes. But it must be due in part to some of the many conditions of the Irish mind that we've considered in this book: our ability to communicate by not saying things, the tensions created by living in small places, emigration, pain, the strange weight of history. Many of our great writers are miniaturists – they can track the tiny emotional shifts between love and resentment, tenderness and loss. Others deal a lot with the past and our relationship with it.

Then why hasn't there been a rush towards writing about the Celtic Tiger and our fall afterwards? Perhaps it's just too soon. Perhaps it is as yet too difficult to portray it as a singular whole. There also has never been much of a tradition of social-realist writing here. In Ireland, the way we live has always been portrayed in disconnected bits, as if the whole was too much to take in.

Or perhaps writing about our recent past will become the job of a subsequent generation of writers. Certainly the current generation doesn't seem to be anywhere close to running out of subject matter.

As for music, Ireland has always been remarkable for the variety of styles it has embraced. The book and movie *The Commitments* was about a soul band in Dublin, and when Garth Brooks sold 400,000 tickets for a series of shows in Croke

Park (subsequently cancelled after a planning fiasco), urban Ireland was reminded just how popular country music is in Ireland. Then there are rock bands, weepy singer-songwriters, boy bands, traditional music. We do spectacularly well because of history and globalisation.

When the Irish emigrated to the US and the UK we brought our music with us, and in the US in particular the echoes of it can still be heard. In 1987, the Emmy-winning TV series *Bringing It All Back Home* traced the influence of this music and where it ended up, from the likes of Elvis Costello to the Everly Brothers.

Many Irish who arrived in the US in the 18th century settled in the Appalachian Mountains, where their music fused with that of other Europeans and Africans and became Old Time music. Old Time directly influenced American country music, bluegrass and rock 'n' roll. One example of this is a traditional Irish song called *The Bard of Armagh* (also known as *The Unfortunate Rake*), which over time evolved into *The Streets of Laredo*, a famous cowboy ballad. That in turn morphed into *St. James Infirmary Blues*, a jazz standard covered by dozens of artists, including Louis Armstrong, Cab Calloway, the White Stripes and, more recently, the actor Hugh Laurie.

The musical connections between Ireland and the United States go back centuries and became apparent all over again during the American folk boom of the 1960s, during which Bob Dylan, among others, championed the Clancy Brothers in the US. We brought music over there, and they sent it back to us. No wonder American country music is so popular in Ireland. It's *Irish* country music, not just in the instruments and rhythms, but in the subjects it talks about – small-town life and that sense of being looked down upon, or ignored, by the city. It's about the urban–rural split.

The musical connections also helped form human ones. Hosts of UK and US artists have come here to explore the music and in doing so have made contacts, which in turn helped Irish musicians of various sorts bring their music to a wider audience. And those foreign, particularly American, audiences responded quickly to this Irish-tinged music – because it sounded like *American* music.

But there's another, perhaps more humdrum, factor: we just do music *more*. In villages, towns and cities across Ireland, ordinary people with no dreams of stardom perform for the weekend crowds in pubs. Young people grow up hearing this, often taking part. Musicianship is normal. Add to that the digital age, when your average 15-year-old can record a song in their bedroom and post it online. Everyone is the next potential Hozier.

This long process of cross-pollination and immersive musicality must even have been a factor in why Ireland has also produced a handful of successful pop acts, a singularly global-ised form of music, almost completely devoid of any national characteristics. That, plus that golden version of ourselves we spoke about earlier. Pop music requires performers with looks and personality, and nobody beats us at personality. It may also explain our run of victories in the Eurovision during the 1990s – until Eastern Europe ruined everything for us.

The only area of art in which the Irish don't seem to do as well – or at least not as well as we do in writing and music – is the visual area. Perhaps due to poverty, there hasn't been as much of a tradition of it. It's not that there haven't been Irish artists of note, or that there aren't Irish artists working now. We seem to be doing as well as you'd expect from a country the size of Ireland. Terry Eagleton puts it quite baldly: 'They [the Irish] are notorious for their lack of a visual sense.'

His evidence for this is not the output from Irish artists, but how we have managed our physical environs. He describes O'Connell Street in Dublin as 'a dingy collection of fast food joints. One critic called its architectural style "neon-classical".'

Ouch. But he may have a point. As Seán Ó Faoláin pointed out, the vast majority of Irish towns were founded by the Danes, the Normans or the Tudors. Terry Eagleton builds on this idea by claiming that the Irish have acted as if the land isn't our own because for many centuries it wasn't. And because of that, we are poor town planners. Just try driving a car around Galway City.

A prime example of this poor planning is the M3 motorway. It had been sorely needed for some time. Young couples with kids, forced to move outside the M50 because of high house prices, found themselves having to make a daily slog between Navan and Dublin on a road that was built for 1950s traffic. A rail link would have helped, but we didn't get that. Instead we got the M3 motorway – except the M3 passed perilously close to the Hill of Tara and right through the archaeologically rich Tara-Skryne Valley. An Bord Pleanála signed off on the scheme – and that particular route – presumably without thinking that anyone would be too bothered about it.

But of course they were. There was a huge stink, which pitted conservationists against tormented commuters who just wanted to get home earlier. The road opened in 2010, though according to a report in the *Irish Independent*, Pagans who worship at Tara claimed that it had created a 'negative energy'. And they were right. The majority of commuters probably wouldn't have wanted the road to pass through an archeologically sensitive area, but any alternative would have involved waiting yet another five years.

We are only just beginning to think of ourselves as an urban people, which is perhaps why we seem to have placed less importance on the layout of towns and cities or indeed what sorts of buildings we live and work in. Just drive through any Irish town or any part of the Irish countryside to see evidence of that poor visual sense. Our houses are horrible.

They are, for the most part, gaudy boxes or triangles. Unless the owner has a few bob and wants to make a statement, in which case the style often tends towards looking like a ranch. The TV show *Dallas* has a lot to answer for.

So does the architect and former Fianna Fáil senator Jack Fitzsimons, who died in 2014. Fitzsimons is the author of *Bungalow Bliss*, first published in 1971 and reprinted 10 times. Essentially, it was a book of house designs – or *one* house design with many variants – along with information on planning laws and how to go about getting a house built. There was a time when it seemed that every home in Ireland had a copy, along with a Bible and a picture of JFK. You can still buy it on Amazon. You can also see the fruits of some of his designs on a Facebook page called Ugly Irish Houses. He's been criticised for enabling the kind of ribbon development that many claim blights the Irish countryside.

But in fairness to Fitzsimons (and he wasn't a man to take criticism lightly), *Bungalow Bliss* was published at a time when architects' fees were outside the reach of most ordinary

Irish families. He did enable a generation of Irish people to construct their own homes. What was more important then, and perhaps now, were the people inside the house, not what it looked like.

Because what hasn't changed in Ireland, at least in terms of its continuing existence, is the family. A study carried out in 2012 found that 62 per cent of Irish people cited family as the biggest influence on their thinking and opinion (so much for the power of the media, which came in at just 33 per cent). The family is still the basic unit of society, and no matter how oddly shaped or dysfunctional or infuriating it might be, the vast majority of us are part of one, and want to be so.

The shape and size and complexion, though – *they* are different. The Irish family has been getting steadily smaller for some time. In 1991 the average family had two children, but by the 2011 census that figure had shrunk to 1.4.

And an awful lot of these kids don't have married parents: over one-third are born outside wedlock. This doesn't mean their parents won't get married, just that the order of life events seems to be changing. In fact, marriage has been increasing in popularity in recent years. But now it seems to be increasingly common to move in together, have the 1.4 kids and then get hitched. In the *Irish Times* family values survey in 2015, opinion was split 50-50 as to whether this makes any difference or not.

Another relatively new development is separation and divorce. Around 6 per cent of couples in Ireland have experienced marital breakdown, and with that the mind-melting complications and tensions involved with who gets the kids and when. It can often be messy, painful and expensive –

and is one area where the rights of fathers need more equitable treatment by the courts.

Yet it's not all tragedy for the divorced. Between 1996 and 2011, the remarriage rate shot up by 550 per cent.

The 2011 census also records 4,042 same-sex co-habiting couples and 3,000 couples who had undergone civil partnerships. They are families too.

The *Irish Times* survey also found a general sense of optimism. In terms of education, quality of life, even financial security, the respondents felt that things are better now than they were in their parents' day. We spend so much time flailing ourselves for our failures that we forget just how far our society has come. And there's no reason to believe that things won't improve even more, not just in material terms, but in the way our children will regard the past and the future – in the way our children will *think*.

Most middle-aged people in Ireland would have had a parent, or more likely a grandparent, who remembered the War of Independence and the Civil War. Like my grandfather, they may well have had an involvement in those events (we'll get to that). It wasn't just history, it was *family* history, shadowed with pain or pride. But to my children, all they know of their great-grandfather, John Reilly, is a man in a faded black-and-white photograph, looking rather pleased with himself, his hat tipped at an angle. From his jacket pocket sticks a rolled-up piece of paper, containing, according to family lore, my Uncle Alfie's matriculation results. But this is just history to them, something that happened in the sepia past.

Being Irish will inevitably feel different to our kids. They may come to live in a world where nationality is less important, at least in the political sense. Some differences are already apparent. For them, the struggle associated with our nationality – the loss, the resentment, the lack of confidence – is fading away.

When I did my Leaving Cert, my parents fiercely resisted my desire to go to Dublin to study journalism, and with the best of intentions. It seemed far too insecure, too unknown. They wanted me to do what everyone else did: join the bank or the civil service, or go to UCG and become a teacher afterwards. What I wanted seemed far too remote and unlikely. Now, when I look back, I have no idea what convinced me that I could succeed.

My children – and yours – suffer from no such restrictions. Rather, their problem is the dizzying weight of choice and of how employment may change in the future. It will be all contracts, they say. No security. They may have to change careers three or four times.

There will always be something to worry about.

They will go out into the world – a much smaller, much more crowded world – and it will be up to them to define, or redefine, Irishness. Because it's not a fixed quality; it never was. And in the course of that redefinition, things will be gained but also lost. They may not be able to hold back all that logical, western thought. The joy of entertaining two contradictory ideas might eventually become an indulgence we can't afford.

They could look back at what their parents failed to do: make being Irish *stand* for something – make Irish not just a description, but an idea. That's easier said than done. We can't transform ourselves into a Nordic or an American country because we're not like them. Our children will have to be realistic about what our strengths and weaknesses are and try to build a fair society around that.

They may ask themselves a simple question: not what does it mean to be Irish, but what would we like being Irish to mean?

Chapter 7

Turkey in the Post: Just Outside of Knowable

In January 2015, Helen and I made a trip to Killala. There was a long-standing invitation to visit our cousins there, and they had told us about a local woman who had known our mother in London. It might answer some of the questions we still had – when she went, why she went.

I had jotted down the list of towns to drive through, but we didn't see half of them. A new road we didn't know about swelled up before us and zipped us past towns and villages that had been part of the mental landscape of our annual holidays: Foxford, Swinford, Balla, Claremorris. It's another way that Ireland has changed. The physical experience of travel was once punctuated by a series of towns and well-known spots to stop off for a cup of tea. Now it's the anonymous European autobahn. You just see signs for the places now, pointing to the past.

We drove along and named these places, and tried to piece together memory shards of drives, trips to the beach and picnics – plastic-tasting tea from a flask. We wondered if the woman we were due to visit would be able to tell us much. Helen wasn't so sure. So much of what we first learned about Ireland came from our mother. But like most things you can say about this country, it was only a version – *her* version, formed by family history, by her temperament, her experience, by what she chose to say and chose to keep silent about. Helen doubted if there was some earlier version of our mother where she was less guarded. Of course not. She was Irish.

She was *so* Irish. We rarely had any glimpse into her interior life; she would deny she had one. For reasons we'll never know, she chose to emigrate, but never seemed to get over it. The sadness was upon her, and an anger too. If taken by the mood, she could be good company, but she was close to impossible to get to know. She was a devoted Catholic, but I always suspected she didn't believe a word of it. When we were children she mythologised Ireland, but when we moved back it seemed to irritate her. She was contrary and contradictory and haunted by history. My Irish paradox.

I tried to remember the last time I had been to Killala. A bad idea: you trace back the years and it's always a shock. Time is devouring everything. It had been at least a decade, for the funeral of our Aunt Bernie. Padraig Flynn had attended, arriving at the last moment to sweep through the church, all black-suited and vampiric. Beverley Cooper-Flynn had also been there and Sharon Shannon had played music (my cousin John Dunford is her manager). The priest had seemed tremendously impressed.

Yet Killala didn't seem that different. Why should it be? The same curved, cosy streets. The round tower. Killala is village-sized, but actually it's a town with an ecclesiastical past stretching back at least 1,500 years. St Patrick baptised 12,000 people here in one day. He raised a man from the dead – or so the story goes. It's a quiet, old place. Life and death, endlessly played out.

We called in to our cousin Steve's house, then ventured out to meet the woman we had come to see. Steve advised us about what pubs to visit and what pubs to avoid, should we feel the need afterwards.

Her name was Patsy, and one of the first memories she relayed to us was of a woman in the town who had been ordered to leave. This was in the 1920s or 1930s. The woman had three children – one of them a baby – and the order was relayed to her by her cousin, who was a member of the IRA. She was told that if she didn't leave, she would be shot. Her crime was that she was married to a member of the RIC.

My grandfather, John Reilly, was also a member of the RIC. According to our mother, he was pensioned off after receiving an injury following an IRA attack, though we don't know when this took place or what the circumstances were. My cousin Chuck gave me John Reilly's 1912 edition of *The Irish Constables Guide*, which covers everything from poaching to challenging someone to fight a duel. I have leafed through it, looking for clues, but found nothing. There are some scribbles, but I think they came from my Uncle Alfie, who would have been a child then. We don't even know if he served as a constable in Killala. He had been previously stationed in Ennis.

Yet in the first few decades of the last century, the Reillys must have lived with the knowledge that there were people in the town who would have killed him had the circumstances been slightly different. They would have regarded him as a traitor. Our mother didn't make friends easily, but on a few occasions over the years she did meet people who were also the children of RIC men, and with them there seemed to be an instant bond, as if borne of a shared injury. They knew what it had been like.

Patsy also remembered when John Reilly died. It was sudden, she said, and she remembered our mother, Alfie and our grandmother, Mary Kate, at the wake. The other siblings, Cathleen and Bernie, were probably too young to go. She recalled too that Alfie had gone to UCD to study medicine, something that had probably caused a minor sensation in the town at the time. To have a doctor in the family was regarded as a major step up, socially speaking, as well as a huge investment. Through Mary Kate's family, the Munnellys (a massive proportion of this part of Mayo seems to have the surname Munnelly), the Reillys had inherited some land and cattle and, a few years later, at least a share in a pub. It was all sold to pay for Alfie's education.

Yet after six years he returned to Killala, still unqualified. The lung condition – sarcoidosis – had become too bad. Patsy could remember Mary Kate or some neighbours sometimes having to stay up all night with him as he coughed and heaved. He did that for the rest of his life.

I'm speculating, but I don't think it's unreasonable to guess at what the local reaction to this might have been. The RIC family, the ones who took the King's shilling, get notions and send the eldest son to be a doctor, no less. And Alfie was the sort of man who you could easily imagine being a magnet for begrudgery – a bit too smart-assed, a bit too well dressed. Over the years a couple of comments had been made, though I never got the subtext. *He spent a lot of time on himself in Dublin. He didn't die wondering.*

Even today, the exact cause of sarcoidosis isn't known. There may be a genetic component, combined with bacterial infection. Yet for some people in Killala at the time, it may have been all too easy and satisfying to assume that he'd brought it on himself. He'd squandered his family's money and was now too idle to complete the last year of university. No doubt everyone knew that he rarely got out of bed before midday. But he couldn't; he didn't sleep.

Alfie spent the rest of his life in Killala, and from what I could see, he did so quite happily. He followed horses, played cards and was involved in several community organisations. He was part of a group who successfully lured showbands to play in Killala in the 1970s.

I can't help but wonder what my mother made of all this at the time – whether the suppressed sniggers, the public *failure* of her family to produce a doctor, made her want to leave. All the money had been spent on her brother.

Actually, not all the money. She took her matriculation examination in Gortnor Abbey, in Crossmolina, a convent school run by the Jesus and Mary order of nuns. She would have been a boarder there for a least a year, and almost certainly did some, if not all, of her subjects through Irish.

I never heard my mother speaking Irish. I never even knew she could.

After that, she taught in Templemary National School in Killala and then moved to Dublin, where she worked as a private tutor. This is one of the ways memory works: someone tells you what they know and it can spark something you'd long forgotten. As Patsy told us about our mother's move to Dublin, Helen recalled something she'd been told years before: that our mother had worked for a diplomat.

But Patsy said she didn't think it was a diplomat. It was Seán T. O'Kelly, though this would have been before he became president. He was probably a government minster at the time.

After that, she went to London. Patsy was unable to tell us when this might have been. Patsy herself went in 1952, and our mother (who was older) had been there for many years at that stage. She had taught in a convent, and later on taught in a school in Enfield, east of London. In Enfield, she had stayed with a family called the Quinlins, who were also from Killala. Mrs Quinlin was a Munnelly.

But at the weekends she would travel into London, and many times stayed with Patsy and some other Killala people who lived in Kentish Town. She was always mad for news from home, Patsy said. Sometimes they went dancing or to the pictures or visited people. Half of the town seemed to be there at the time. It was an Ireland where a large family was the norm, so a few out of every house emigrated. They'd often head to Hyde Park, around Speakers' Corner, and find Killala people sitting on the grass.

We asked if she ever had any boyfriends, but Patsy couldn't remember. She never brought anyone around our way. She was quiet, Patsy said.

Because she was teaching, she was able to go back to Killala for a long stretch every summer, usually in possession of a list of orders. Rationing was still in effect, so our mother would return laden down with tea and eggs and bacon.

Patsy grew tired then, so we said our goodbyes and thank yous. On the way back up to Steve's house, Helen remembered another story: that one Christmas, Mary Kate Reilly had sent us a turkey. She had posted it. It had taken a week to get to London, and by the time it arrived, the bird had turned a fungal, vivid green.

That night we sat around Steve's dinner table overlooking Killala Bay and wondered at the many gaps still left in the story. It was amazing, but also typical, that she had never mentioned teaching the kids of an Irish government minister. But a quick Google search quickly smashed that fascinating prospect. Seán T. O'Kelly was married twice, but never had any children. So it was a diplomat – or perhaps not.

But then another fragment came back to Steve. One night, he had bumped into a man in a local pub – a man he had known for many years and who would have been a contemporary of our mother. He asked after her, and then said, 'I was madly in love with Molly.'

This man was from a generation that didn't make declarations like this. It was so surprising, and so heartfelt, that it took Steve by surprise. It wasn't some secret attraction either. It seemed as if there had been a real love story, one with a beginning and an end.

'I followed her to London,' the man said, 'but she rejected me.'

Steve was so taken aback, he didn't ask him any more about it that night. He promised himself he would again, but he never had the chance; the man died soon after.

Needless to say, our mother had never mentioned this. It's not the sort of thing you divulge to your kids, I suppose. Perhaps the attraction wasn't mutual. Or perhaps she knew she couldn't go back, even then.

We will never discover all our mother's secrets. Like the country she came from, she remained just outside of knowable.